W9-DCG-166

The sacraments

Thoughtful reflections for catechists

THE
Sacraments

*Thoughtful Reflections
for Catechists*

FR. HALBERT WEIDNER

Cover: Bread and cup image ©iStockphoto/Zuki

TWENTY-THIRD PUBLICATIONS
A Division of Bayard
One Montauk Avenue, Suite 200
New London, CT 06320
(860) 437-3012 or (800) 321-0411
www.23rdpublications.com

ISBN 978-1-58595-740-8
Library of Congress Catalog Card Number: 2009940855
Printed in the U.S.A.

CONTENTS

Introduction

As a catechist you are essential to parish ministry, but you are also part of a busy world. I wrote this book to support catechists who would like a handy, brief sketch of some of the essentials of what they are about when they share their faith and sacramental practice.

Catechesis is a science and an art. As a catechist you are both a guide and a cook. Catechesis, like cooking, is meant to feed hearts, minds, and souls. Without a cook the recipes may make great reading but fail the starving reader. As you make your journey as a catechist and encounter many things, this book is meant to help you keep the main lines straight. Only you, the catechist, can provide the wonderful details that make faith sharing really come alive.

But what to do after the meal is cooked and shared? Perhaps another image for this little book is that of a compass. Catechesis is meals on wheels. We are a people on the move. The journey with Christ is from darkness and slavery through the desert and then into the promised land of Easter. The needle of our catechetical compass should always point in that direction.

In each chapter, therefore, there is a brief introduction to some sacramental essentials, including the words and actions that are part of the liturgical celebration, but which could always use more contemplation. With each sacrament there is a section for reflection and questions. Though brief, this book is meant to enrich your understanding and help you connect the sacraments to your life. Of course, God has never been out of your life; the doctrine is always living.

This ministry entrusted to you by the Church feeds you, the cook, and all the people invited by the Lord to the table. May Jesus, who formed a people around a table—may Jesus the Living Water—raise you and yours up to eternal life. May the Holy Spirit, through Jesus, bring you and yours to the Father!

Baptism

Can you remember your first day of school? Your first date? Your first day on the job?

Your experiences will help you teach baptism because baptism is about new beginnings, the death of the old, the shock of the new. If you remember the shock of these deaths/new beginnings you will capture something very important about the sacrament of baptism.

Water, fire, and new beginnings

In the life of the Jewish community the Passover mystery is central, and we get our experience of baptism from these people of the first covenant. They start out from slavery led by Moses, with the army of Pharaoh right behind them, and then they run up against a huge body of water blocking their way. They go through it! That is the very definition of a new beginning. When Jesus is baptized, dunked in the waters of the Jordan by John, he repeats the experience of Israel going through the waters. We know this for sure because, right after, he continues the journey by going out into the desert just as Israel did. The shock of a new beginning is just that—a new beginning. It is *not* arrival. Everyone getting baptized is just beginning, but what a beginning!

We have lots of images of shocking new beginnings. People will talk about going through a baptism of fire. Soldiers certainly do, but anyone who has tried to do something new gets scorched too. In baptism, the fire is real. It is the fire of the Holy Spirit. It burns away something but also creates something new.

But baptism is supposed to be about water! It is about water, but it is also about fire.

Saint Thérèse, the "Little Flower," who is portrayed usually as someone rather fragile and sweet, said, "I would go through fire to get to Jesus." You are inviting your young Christians to do the same.

I used to live and teach in Hawaii. These islands are really huge mountains, huge volcanoes that spewed fire and molten lava under water. Finally an island appeared above water: a new beginning out of water and fire. Baptism is, if anything, more dramatic, more thrilling. A fragile human being is united to God. It is the whole story of creation all over again, only this time the Holy Spirit re-creates a human being. Easter is Day One. Baptism is the sacrament of Day One.

A complete transformation

Before we go any further, please look at these two samples from prayers used at baptism: "We pray for these children; set them free from original sin, make them temples of your glory, and send your Holy Spirit to dwell within them." Another prayer in the ritual says that Jesus "gives us the freedom only [God's] sons and daughters enjoy." Are these just words? Can you see the freedom that flows out of the baptized? Can you see the young people in front of you in their "glory"?

Nothing compares to baptism. We can join a club, become a citizen of another country, change political parties, become famous, but nothing will ever come close to the transformation caused by being baptized. We could even go to the depths of hell, as far from God as we possibly could will ourselves, but it would not change the reality that we are baptized and that baptism changed the person we are, even if we do not want to be that person. We are all created by God, but after baptism we have been re-created.

That re-creation, that transformation, that kind of radical evolution—that is the heart of teaching baptism and continues on through all the other sacraments. There is a prayer that reminds us of this that is said by the priest silently at Mass when he adds the water to the wine in the chalice: "By the mystery of this water and wine may we come to share in the divinity of Christ who humbled himself to share in our humanity." It is in baptism that we first come to share in the divinity of Jesus, who commanded us to make disciples and baptize them in the name of the Father, the Son, and the Holy Spirit.

Creating divine life

Baptism is the sacrament of beginning, and once we begin, we can try to turn back, but God will never un-baptize us. We are always changed by this sacrament. We are always baptized. Often we might say, "I *was* baptized." Instead we should say, "I *am* baptized." Sometimes baptism was said to confer an "indelible mark." But it is much more than that, of course, because it is the irrevocable creation of divine life in us. That's why baptism is unrepeatable. Once created, we cannot do anything to un-create ourselves. Once re-created, we cannot do anything to reverse it. Hell is possible for sure, if human freedom means anything, but the gate is locked from inside. God never once gave up on us, never reversed the creation and the re-creation that made us who we are before God and in God.

Baptism is so important, it is the only sacrament that can be conferred by a non-baptized person. Anyone can baptize if they have the intention to do what the Church intends and they say the words using the name of the Trinity. We should meditate on the fact that the two sacraments that sustain most of the Church most of the time are either not conferred by clergy (marriage) or need not be conferred by clergy (baptism). These two great sacraments have sustained the Church in the darkest times of persecution not only when clergy were scarce, but when no other structures in the Church survived except the family.

Beyond the signs of washing

Baptism in the New Testament is a word that means dunking or immersing. That practice never was given up in the eastern or Byzantine churches. It can shock a western Catholic to attend a baptism where the child is really dunked. But the shock is good for us because it reminds us of something that the celebrant prays: "We ask you, Father, with your Son to send the Holy Spirit upon the water of this font. May all who are buried with Christ in the death of baptism rise also with him to the newness of life." Besides "washing," the water is a sign of dying and rising to new life.

As a former Southern Baptist, I can tell you that my baptism was something dramatic and easily remembered: Down the steps into the tank and down into the water I went, with one of my pastor's strong arms behind my head and the other behind my shoulder. Down I went and up I came. I can close my eyes and feel that all over again even though it was decades ago. I really did feel, as a dunked Southern Baptist, the dying and rising to new life that the Catholic prayer speaks about.

For the last thirty years at Easter, adults being baptized in the Catholic Church get the chance to experience this dramatic dying and rising in water. Some lucky babies get the same chance in the western Church because the rite (since 1969) calls for immersion as the first option. After all, baptism in Greek means to dunk. Of course, this dramatic action impacts the community more than the baby, who will not remember it, but it is good for the community to see this dying and rising to new life. At children's liturgies and Sunday Masses, the reality of baptism often sinks into the hearts of people when they are confronted with more than a little pouring of water, a little dab of oil, the usual abbreviations and shortcuts of a once-rich celebration of splendidly clear and generous elements provided by God's creation.

From day one to the last day

Baptism is the sacrament of letting go, leaving behind, plunging into a reality that only faith sustains. That is to say, it is like death! All catechists should know that this reality of dying and rising to new life certainly comes roaring back at funerals. At baptism, we were anointed with chrism so we might "live always as members of his body, sharing everlasting life." This baptismal prayer and many others that speak of "everlasting life" show how related the baptismal rite is to the funeral rite.

So at baptism we receive the white garment, the sign of new creation, which comes with the admonition that the dignity we receive at baptism be brought—with the word and example of family and friends—into the everlasting life of heaven. In the same way, the last white garment we receive will be the pall covering our coffin. Rich or poor, expensive or not so expensive, the coffin gets hidden under the white covering, a sign of our baptism. We are, by baptism, all equal, all hidden in Christ.

Then there is a presentation of a lighted candle. We light this small candle for the newly baptized from the Easter Candle, the light of Christ shining in the darkness of death. This Easter candle also will be at the funeral, burning brightly up front. And the prayer at baptism is: "may these children keep the flame of faith alive in their hearts. When the Lord comes, may they go out to meet him with all the saints in the heavenly kingdom." When the saints go marching in we hope to be in that number. The sacrament of baptism is the sacrament of beginnings, and when we arrive at the end of the beginning, and begin the ending, then we shall rejoice to say, "I am baptized."

FOR REFLECTION AND DISCUSSION

1. What experiences have you had that helped you appreciate the natural, life-giving power of water? What has happened in your life that helped you understand how dangerous water can be? Even if you are not a morning person, can you see the dawn as an experience of creation being invited back just as it was on the "first day"?

2. We experience water as something safe and easily available, but what else is necessary but not safe, not easily found? What has this necessity got to do with baptism?

3. What experiences have you had that were beginnings? What were your first experiences of friendship? What impact have children had on your life?

4. Granted that babies always draw our attention, what experiences of infant baptism have meant the most to you? What adult baptisms have you been a part of? How have you shared these experiences with others?

5. Have you been at the funeral of an infant or known someone whose child has died? How has your faith influenced your response?

6. What experiences of funerals have impacted you the most? Did any of the baptismal symbols at the Catholic funerals communicate something?

PRAYER

Let the glory of your life, O God, shine in us always, but especially now as we prepare to share our faith in what you have done to make us your own in the life of the Church. Even when the darkness is very dark and sin threatens your children, let us take refuge in the glory given us in Jesus, the light of the world. Help us to keep the light you have given us shining through until we meet the Lord with all the angels and saints in the heavenly kingdom. We ask this, Father, in the name of Jesus by the power of the Holy Spirit.

Eucharist

As a catechist, imagine if you and all the persons you share your faith with had hurried to escape from a land of slavery and brutal death. If you had celebrated a meal together on the night before you were liberated by the power of God, that meal would stand out and be celebrated at least every year on the anniversary of your escape.

If you added to this experience a Jewish idea of prayer—that remembering and thanking God for what was done to liberate people, and believing that this remembering is a way to make the event present to a generation that came long after—you would have the foundations of a good theology of Eucharist.

The original Eucharist, the Last Supper, where Jesus took bread and wine, was in the Passover tradition, celebrating the escape from Egypt. The bread—unleavened because there was no time for bread to rise—and the cup of blessing—a foretaste of freedom and joy—are Jewish experiences that have come to us through Jesus. The celebration's compass needle points fast and hard away from death, which flies overhead and which will pursue the people right to the shores of a sea that must part if freedom and not destruction is to come to them.

Doing what Jesus did

One of the great privileges you have as a catechist is to share your faith in the Eucharist—the summit, the high point of Catholic life. For nearly two thousand years the Church has, in various ways but in every time and place, baptized people and gathered them to celebrate the Eucharist. It will continue to do this until the end of time. Now, you gather young ones around you so that they too can begin to grasp—and to be grasped by—the great mystery we call the Eucharist.

We start our understanding sitting by Jesus the night before he died. It is Passover time, the celebration that marks the new beginning of the Jewish people and their journey from slavery to freedom. Now Jesus begins his own Passover from death to life. He takes a cup of wine and a flat piece of Passover bread. He says a blessing. For a Jew, a blessing prayer is a blessing not of the bread and wine but of God. A blessing prayer in the Jewish tradition is a prayer of thanksgiving. And by giving thanks, we make the thing we are thankful for present in God. "Blessed are you, Lord God, because...." But then after the prayer of blessing, Jesus gives his disciples the bread and the cup, saying: "Take this all of you and eat. This is my body. Take this, all of you, and drink. This is my blood." And then Jesus says one more thing very new: "Do this in remembrance of me."

When we do what Jesus did, we celebrate the Eucharistic liturgy: We take bread, we take a cup of wine, we pray the blessing prayer, including repeating Jesus' words over the bread and wine, and we break the bread and share the cup in remembrance of Jesus. The children before you can see and hear these simple and profound actions of Jesus. They will understand at least the minimum required by the Church: that this bread and wine are no longer ordinary, and that the friend they instinctively trust is doing something special for them.

Immersed in Jesus' death and resurrection

This action of Jesus, this simple faith of his followers, continues in the Church today. While we could not be present at the Last Supper and the giving of Jesus' life on the cross, that unrepeatable death is made present to us here and now. We could not be present at the resurrection, but that unrepeatable Easter is made present to us here and now. We could not be there for the ascension, but when we remember Jesus, all of the life-giving actions of Jesus are made present to us.

This reality, as I have said, comes to us from the Jewish faith. In the Jewish faith, to remember by blessing God in prayer is to make present. At the Passover the child asks, "Why is tonight different from all other nights?" And the answer is "because tonight the Lord God takes us out of Egypt." The word is *now*, the word is *tonight*. By remembering we make present, really present. We remember in a special way, and we pray what we remember. We say, "Blessed are you, Lord God, *because...*" and then we tell God the story of what God has done and we bless God for the blessings given us in what God has done. For the Christian child, the Eucharist is the special way of remembering Jesus, joining in the offering of Jesus to the Father, where we ourselves and our gifts of bread and wine are transformed into Christ and given back to us in Holy Communion. Of course, books have been written about each phrase I just used, but the essentials are there in these few words. We can spend the rest of our lives living them out.

Sharing a meal

The dynamics you need to share with the children are the dynamics of the Passover—Jesus leads us to eternal life out of the slavery of sin and death. But the dynamics you need to share are also present in simple home meals. Home experiences of meals will probably be something everyone can share in. You may not be able to convey much about great dramatic things like sin and death, but you certainly can use your own experiences to give color to your words and body to your gratitude. The children will hear that.

The power of sharing in a meal is overwhelming. In America, a nation of immigrants, we often forget the original languages of our families. We sometimes forget (we are so bad at geography) where the original country was. What we don't forget is the food! You can lead your sessions with the young people by opening the Yellow Pages to the restaurant section or by photocopying the section and sharing reactions. The young people may have their own favorite foods and stories about the special foods ("ethnic," but who isn't ethnic?) from their family history. Some of your children may only see the food. But other, wiser children will know what you mean when you say that the love of the ones who made and cooked the meal have transformed both the food and the eating into something special.

God does this too—to the maximum in the Eucharist. Jesus calls his family to a table where the Spirit—the Spirit of Jesus, the Spirit of the God who is love—transforms food for bodies into food for bodies and souls. The Holy Spirit transforms the bread and wine into something very special. And because what we receive is utterly changed, we can be utterly changed too.

A sacrificial meal

This meal is also called a sacrifice. You need a little background to realize that you understand this already. The prophets used to complain that the animal sacrifices of the Temple were no good if the worship was just lip service. Eventually the Temple was torn down, the priesthood suspended, and the people taken off to a foreign land. The prophets now said that the people had to learn to offer not the sacrifices of animals, but the sacrifice of their hearts, the sacrifice of genuine thanksgiving and praise.

Jesus did that. He offered his whole self, his whole heart to God. He offered the sacrifice of praise, and the Father accepted it. Now we who are baptized into Christ and living in him, offer ourselves in Christ. And the Spirit makes of this offering a genuine thanksgiving, a real thanksgiving from the heart. "Eucharist" is Greek for thanksgiving.

This prayer of thanksgiving, the Eucharistic prayer, means that the Mass is more than a Communion service. We can have a Communion service without a priest. We need consecrated Hosts and someone to lead the service. But without a priest leading the Eucharistic liturgy, we cannot offer up ourselves in the Eucharist as thanksgiving united in the offering of Jesus.

The power of the priest is not just to say the words of Jesus that transform the gifts into the real presence of Christ, but it is also the power of Christ in the priest to lead the people in communion with the whole Church in offering the Eucharist. If we read the Eucharistic prayers carefully we can get an idea of what is going on and why a Communion service cannot replace the Mass.

Understanding the real presence

We must be careful to understand the real presence of Christ in the Eucharist. Christ is really present in either of the consecrated elements. So a sick person who may not be able to eat but could receive from the cup would receive the entire Christ. Ideally, we should receive Christ present under the appearances of both bread and wine, but we do not divide Christ, who is risen and present under the appearances of either.

This can be confusing because liturgical language preserves the original words without explanation or changes. These words must be explained by catechists because the language of the liturgy is unchanging and spare. Christ is really present in the Eucharist even though what we can see and touch does not change. In discussing baptism, we said the person baptized is transformed. That could be hard to see. Now we're saying that the bread and wine are transformed, and that is impossible to see. But we can still understand it.

For instance, even on the human scale we know that physical presence is not necessarily real presence or human presence. We can be as intimate physically as we can be with another person but still be absent humanly. For example, a college student going, say, into her chemistry class, gets a text message from her beloved—what we used to call a love note and which used to be on paper. What happens? The student goes into class and gets a seat as far back as possible. She sits down, props a textbook or laptop in front of her, and opens the text message. Who is present? Is the teacher present? Or is it the beloved? It is, of course, the beloved. Real presence does not, cannot depend on physical presence. Neither is it just psychological. And when the words of Jesus and the work of the Holy Spirit convey the real presence, we can believe that it is not just psychological, not just our imagination or our faith, but an objective presence, a real presence.

So the bread and wine are transformed at Mass not physically but really. In the philosophical language used by the Church, we say the bread and wine are changed substantially. And Christ is really present, though no physical evidence is there. This is a very serious aspect of our faith, and we should be very careful to avoid so-called miracles where the host or the wine turns to physical flesh or blood. We receive the Lord as he is now, whole and entire, in glory. The Catechism makes this very plain. If we want miracles at Mass, the presence of the saints and the reconciliation of sinners that bless the Church should be enough.

For an example of a miracle of love, we can turn to a story Sister José Hobday told. When she was a little girl her mother loaded her up with a basket of goodies to visit a poor woman whose face was torn into by cancer. José hated to visit her because of the smell and the woman's disfiguration. One year José's parents invited the women to share their Thanksgiving dinner, and José revolted. She said she would not attend if *that* woman was there. Fine, said her mother, and so José had to face a day without food: Dinner was not part of the Hobday family room-service. So, of course, José gave in. Then Mrs. Hobday put José right across from the sick woman at the table. José said the woman looked at her with great kindness and love. She thought José loved her. Well, José did. She gave in not only by granting everyone her physical presence, but her real presence, too.

That meal is what we would call a "meal and a sacrifice." Christ was present there, and when José went to Mass, she received the Eucharist in a deeper and more religious way. Christ, of course, is always present, but we need to be present too.

FOR REFLECTION AND DISCUSSION

1. A Eucharistic church is a community of people who are giving thanks. Write down three things a day each day for a month that you are glad happened. This is what you bring to the Eucharist. What do you think of your list?

2. What kind of bread do you like? What kind of bread do the children eat? Do you know how bread is made? Have you ever seen wheat fields? Have the children? How can you move their experiences out of the store and the fast food restaurant?

3. Real grape juice, not the pasteurized kind, is delicious and, at that stage, non-alcoholic. It is called must. What can you do to experience the making of real grape juice? Some cultures use must regularly in cooking. Is there anyone in the parish who does this and can share some with the children?

4. What kind of suppers have you attended? What made them so special, so easy to remember? Did any of them speak to you of the presence of God? How?

5. Have any of the children been at a children's Mass? What was different about it? Did they like it? When the children have been at Mass with their families, were there some special times they remember? Who were with the children besides their mother or father? Did it make a difference if a favorite relative or friend of the family was with them? Why do they remember this?

6. If the children are at the parish Mass, what can they usually see? Where do they sit? What do they sing? If they go to communion, what is the host like? Do they receive from the cup?

7. Have you ever read the special Eucharistic prayers for children's Masses? How are they different?

8. If the effects of baptism, the transformation of a person into a child of God, are difficult to see, the transformation of the gifts of wine and bread is even more of a challenge.

Pope Benedict helped out some children he met by talking about electricity. You cannot see it, but you can see what it does! There are actually lots of things like that in daily life. Make your list and ask for help from your children to enlarge it.

9. Children, if they get a chance to see the altar at Mass, are usually very good at some kind of creative work. Sometimes they even have a favorite song. See what they can do about describing the Mass, and arrange their work as festively as possible in the room you are using, or in the hall or the entrance of the church. Don't put anything too high up!

PRAYER

Thank you, God, for setting us free from sin and death. Thanks for the strength you give us as we serve you. Thank you for all the love in our lives, for all the freedom you give us. Help us to join together at Mass to offer you our hearts, joined to the heart of Jesus. May the Spirit that transforms the bread and wine into the real presence of Christ help us to give Jesus to a world hungry for him and longing for the freedom of the kingdom of God. Amen.

Reconciliation

After his baptism Jesus headed for the desert and temptation. He experienced the temptation of shortcuts that would short-circuit his mission but get him glory and power. He does not fall for it, and in him we conquer the worst temptations that we as individuals and as Church can experience. But this liberation is sometimes too much for us.

When Moses led the people out of Egypt, they immediately started complaining, and many wanted to go back to the security of slavery. They had a terrifying experience of liberation, but it was not enough to keep them trudging through the desert to the Promised Land so far away and unseen.

It's the same for us. In the chapter on baptism and the transformation that this sacrament effects, we could not be blamed if we said from time to time, "I don't see the transformation." You and I always face the temptation to go back to Egypt and be enslaved to sin.

A deep need to begin again

And so the reconciliation that the Church accepted as its mission gradually took the shape of a post-baptismal rite that could be repeated and repeated as needed. And, in fact, throughout history, individuals have fallen plenty of times and each time needed the sacrament in a serious way. So while the compass we are looking at points to the Promised Land and the experience of living in the risen Lord even now, we still fail and fail again and need to renew the liberating experience of leaving Egypt.

The early Church expected baptism to be the sacrament of reconciliation and that this profound experience would destroy the problem of serious sin. Of course, that was not what happened. Gradually, a public confession and reconciliation emerged. This is still the case in Protestant churches that do not have a ceremony of private confession and reconciliation. The result, though, is drastic: We've all seen the public confessions of some popular television evangelists who sinned seriously.

Both Protestant and Catholic communities know that sin is personal but the effects are public. The Catholic communities eventually found a way to meet Christ in the sacrament of reconciliation by confessing serious sin to a priest or bishop, who speaks not only for God but for the Church. In this sacrament, therefore, we are reconciled both to God and the community.

Teaching the heart of the sacrament

As a catechist, you have the mission of preparing young people in the lifelong need of reconciliation. They will certainly be tempted in their own time and ways to go back to the slavery Jesus wants to lead them out of.

When I get a chance to lead a first reconciliation service, I must confess (no pun intended) that I never vary the gospel or the talk. I always use the gospel of the lost sheep, the one out of 100 that the shepherd goes looking for. Now, lots of people say that this will not work because the children do not know sheep or shepherds. This is often true. But they do know marshmallows, and, like sheep, marshmallows are white. So…

I get 100 marshmallows in bags and two big glass bowls. I then have the children count with me one by one as I put the marshmallows—up to 99—in one big glass bowl. And then I put the last one, number 100, all by itself in an equally large bowl. And then I ask, "If you had 99 marshmallows in one big bowl, would you bother to go look for one more?" Of course, they would not. Ninety-nine marshmallows look like plenty.

The whole experience of the sacrament of reconciliation is that God is a powerful searcher for the lost. God loves that solitary one who is all alone and lost. Children get frightened when they sin, when they "mess" up. They think they must hide, or hide their offense or deny it. The sacrament is a wonderfully safe, warm place where they can find out how much God loves them.

With your help, as the children grow in faith, they will learn to see that accidents or doing unpopular things are not sins.

They will see that freedom is the condition for responsibility. They will learn to think about the values of Jesus as their guideline, not the values of society. Stories of people standing against the crowd are very important. People being punished for doing good will help the children move beyond reward and punishment as motivators.

Your work with parents is very important

Most of the conflicts in the early years between parents and children center around autonomy issues. God wants us to grow up, so God is on the side of the child who wants to grow up. That is painful for catechists and parents at times, but the Holy Spirit will help everyone with the gift of wisdom. Wisdom helps us to keep gospel values while slowly learning to confront new situations with joy and creativity.

During a common celebration of reconciliation, you should be prepared for some parents who have been long absent from this sacrament to approach the priest. The atmosphere created by parents and catechists working on this sacrament together is incredibly healing, and some parents will take advantage of the beautiful ritual to respond themselves.

For catechists working with older children and adults, you may also want to note that the format for the celebration of penance has changed some in theory, but not much in practice. Ideally, an individual preparing for the sacrament has done some reflection and even chosen a Scripture passage for his or her own confession. The priest can supply a passage, but it is a blessing if our young people have enough familiarity with the Bible to do this themselves.

A new beginning

The words of absolution for western Catholics are profound. They say that it is not an angry God that must be reconciled to us, but it is we who must be reconciled to the loving Holy God.

The prayer is clear: "God the Father of mercies through the death and resurrection of his Son has reconciled the world to himself and sent the Holy Spirit among us for the forgiveness of sins; through the ministry of the Church may God give you pardon and peace, and I absolve you in name of the Father and the Son and of the Holy Spirit. Amen."

There could be no better expression or experience of Jesus, no better experience of the Good News, than what is expressed in these words. Most Catholics were babies when baptized, so these words are the renewal of the transformation of baptism, a proclamation, a reality, to which we can say, Amen.

FOR REFLECTION AND DISCUSSION

1. Reward and punishment as motives are a stage of development for children. Many adults get stuck there, and this accounts for the problems we all face in a world that is very far from the one God intended. In this sacrament we get a chance to move away from fear. You could show pictures of children in some of kind of trouble and have the

young people talk to you about what they think is going on. Or you and the children could role play accidents or problems. The ones who play the mom or dad will give you great insights.

2. Affection and safety are the foundations for a child ready to accept God as forgiving. Explore ways your team of catechists can make sure that the children feel safe as well as loved.

3. Within safe limits, tell the children about times you "messed up" as a child and were forgiven. Perhaps there were funny parts to this story that will help the young people laugh at some of the situations they get themselves into.

4. You may have children whose families were refugees from tragic situations. You could have grandparents or relatives who suffered much from others because of race or religion or nationality. The children will have heard some of these stories. How did reconciliation happen in these events?

5. Without much reference to divisions, you could share a lot about reconciliation through pictures, videos, or stories that simply depict children from all kinds of backgrounds being together.

PRAYER

Gather us into your heart, loving God, as friends forever. Help us to forgive and accept forgiveness. Create unity from all our different gifts, especially the gift of reconciliation. Amen.

Confirmation

Privileged with the first covenant, the Jewish people experienced a lot of the Spirit of God. The Scriptures saw the Spirit present right from the beginning of creation. The prophets were filled with the Spirit and spoke of the mystery of the suffering servant. They spoke of the Spirit anointing a prophet of justice and freedom when the day of the Lord had come. Jesus uses these same readings to proclaim who he is.

The Spirit of the Lord is upon Jesus and upon us who are living in Jesus. Like the effects of baptism, this can be hard to see. When the Jewish people were led by Moses—with a fiery pillar going ahead of them during the night and a luminous cloud by day—there was still a fear that held them back. Jesus experiences the Spirit and the fear. And so do we.

The compass tells us that the direction we go with Jesus requires that we turn to a constant renewal of the Spirit and keep our eyes on the prize. The obstacles are obvious in the life of Jesus and in our own lives as well. Still, there is within us a

Spirit-given desire to launch ourselves into the adventure that will leave slavery behind and bring us to the kingdom of God. Human beings are created for growth. We grow through events that look like disasters, or, as the preacher said, "brilliant opportunities, brilliantly disguised." If there is anything that the young people around you want it is to grow up. If there is anything that they are afraid of, it is growing up. Confirmation for them will be the way the Spirit renews and strengthens them for the growth God wants for all of us. Like the sacrament of reconciliation, confirmation can continue the transformation that was decisively begun at baptism.

Completing their initiation

Most baptisms in the early Church were of adults or near adults. Even the children of Christians were known to put off their baptisms until they were far into adulthood. Now we have quite a different experience in the Church. Young people baptized as babies face long lives in a very complicated world. I once asked some high school students, "Do you know why the Church wants to confirm you?" There were a lot of answers, but the one I liked the most was, "Because we will need it!" Indeed.

Confirmation is a sacrament of initiation that helps complete membership in the Church. In the East, confirmation is routinely part of infant initiation. By the way, because this ancient practice continues in the Catholic Byzantine churches, you must be especially careful not to enroll a Byzantine Catholic in your parish confirmation program. Check the papers of baptism to make sure that the candidate is not a

Byzantine Catholic who may be attending a western Catholic parish (very likely due to the absence of a Byzantine Catholic parish church). Confirmation can only be administered once, and for these Catholics that happened at baptism.

As for western Catholics, if an infant or young child is in danger of death in our tradition, confirmation not only can be administered, but should be. And of course, all children of catechetical age being received into the Church should receive the sacraments of initiation in the order of baptism, confirmation, and Eucharist, and usually in one liturgy. And a child of catechetical age should not receive first penance because baptism is for the forgiveness of sins! If the child has been baptized in another church already, then initiation proceeds with lenten penance and at Easter with confirmation and Eucharist. It is very important that these children not be deprived of experiencing the sacraments of initiation this way. It would also be a great teaching moment for the parish.

But for most of those you teach, confirmation comes after baptism, first penance, and Eucharist. That is our practice, and there is some practical sense to this. Certainly most parish programs depend on the desire of parents and their cooperative sons and daughters for this last round of initiation. There is a healthy instinct here, a desire to leave behind childish things, a passion for growing up. And despite all the problems over autonomy issues, most certainly God wants us to grow up.

Part of our re-creation in Christ

Remembering that the sacrament is not exactly a sacrament of adulthood, but a completion of initiation, we can be assured that the gifts of the Holy Spirit can always deepen and grow. Confirmation is a once-in-a-lifetime sacrament upon which to draw until we die. The image of a seal or an indelible mark is used because we want to remember that this sacrament is, like baptism, given only once. God gives us the gift and it is never taken back. So the minister of confirmation calls by name the one receiving the sacrament and says, "Be sealed with the gift of the Holy Spirit." The confirmed one says, of course, "Amen." Then, most beautifully, the minister says, as the risen Lord did, "Peace be with you." And the newly confirmed wishes that same peace, the peace beyond understanding, as a gift also to the bishop or priest.

The Spirit that created the world, and recreated God's people in Christ, is still creating us. The world that is still hostile to God will eventually lose out to the coming kingdom of God. We are part of that kingdom and need the gifts of the Holy Spirit to share in the mission that God has given us. The traditional list adapted from the Jewish prophet Isaiah—wisdom, understanding, right knowledge, courage, reverence, wonder and awe before the Lord—describes some of the dynamics that cannot be contained by words alone. These dynamic qualities, which the saints both canonized and un-canonized demonstrate, make the Church and shake up church people. God knows the chosen get frozen from time to time. God knows that the dynamic of history, and all its cultural changes, needs a people who love and have cast out fear. That is the final gift of confirmation.

Life in the Spirit

The young people around you are more aware than ever of creation and the Spirit of God in nature. They also understand that things need a good environment and time to grow. The things that nature needs are part of the ecology of confirmation, only on a deeper, more human, more spiritual level—as free gifts from God.

Bringing yourself and the young people to a great awareness of the Holy Spirit, the creative Spirit (*Veni Creator Spiritus* in the old hymn), guarantees that you as the catechist and they as your faith community will be happy. It's also a call for some serious pastoral care when you have young people around you who are beaten down and cynical. We also should be alert to affirm young people who are sensitive to suffering and want to do something about it. The traditional way of doing this was to pray for the coming of the creator Spirit and then take on work for the kingdom. Young people all over the world like doing the work of the Spirit. It is tough work, it is grown-up work, and at the same time it is an escape from a childish boredom that they were never meant to endure in the first place.

I once asked a group of young people to describe a friend. They covered a large piece of poster paper with their descriptions. Then I showed them a film about Mother Teresa of Calcutta. And I asked them if Mother Teresa fit the description of a friend. They were sure she did except for one area: being "fun at parties!" But, fortunately, there was a scene in the film showing Teresa at a party receiving young sisters. She was laughing and radiant with joy. So Mother Teresa, full of the Holy Spirit, was even fun at parties. Jesus, full of the Holy

Spirit, was rejected as much for his joy as for his call to justice. Confirmed Christians can be known not only for their courage, but also for the ability to rejoice. It is good to give God thanks and praise.

FOR REFLECTION AND DISCUSSION

1. Adulthood is not all joy and parties, but adults are sustained in their sorrows, perhaps after a long period of darkness and suffering. Are you able to name that gift that sustains adult Christians? Tell some stories about being sustained.

2. The young people you teach can also suffer, and many do. What does the Spirit do for them? How do you and the rest of the Church help?

3. If the children have pets, you may get some wonderful stories out of them about the joy and healing that animals bring to them. What in nature makes you think God's Spirit is still here and that God is not finished with us yet?

4. Are there meaningful, immediate Christian service tasks that the young people of your parish can participate in?

5. Children often take on a special name at confirmation. You will have to be ready for some creative responses. Be ready for the young people to enjoy this looking around

for a new name. It has nothing essential to do with the sacrament, but the chance for a new name does communicate something of a rededication.

6. The Spirit leads us to service and a chance of suffering. The Spirit leads us to celebrate especially weddings, babies, and feast days. Ask the Spirit to give you balance but also not to be afraid of being thrown off balance—by that same Holy Spirit!

7. A popular phrase these days is "game changer." How is the Holy Spirit a game changer in your life, in the life of the young people in your ministry? Why does the Church need the Holy Spirit? What are the dangers of a frozen Church? What are the dangers of change just to be fashionable? How do we discern the Holy Spirit in the changes of our lives?

8. In our tradition the bishop is the usual minister of confirmation. How can you introduce the work of the bishop and the needs he serves in the local church?

9. The parents of the young people in parish programs are often suffering from too many commitments. Can you share your faith with them without adding to burdens that may be too much already?

10. Your most creative children will not always be affirmed. How can you pay attention to the new world that these special children can see?

PRAYER

Holy Spirit, creative Spirit, you are the gift of our loving Father. You lead us to Jesus and, with Jesus, you lead us to the great light and love that made us, keeps us, and will be our eternal life always. Help us to see our mission and to be happy in service. We want to be children of the light and follow Jesus. Amen.

Anointing of the Sick

Anything that holds us back, discourages us, or brings our spirits low is an invitation to give up and go back to Egypt. Sickness is the most common experience of this. In times past, sickness was often understood to be the result of sin and faintheartedness. We would not say that today, but we know how badly sickness of mind, body, and soul afflict us. We join in a kind of passion of Christ in these unmerited moments of affliction.

As the Israelites left Egypt, there must have been sick persons among the people. This must have worried Moses. Prophets were supposed to heal and restore sick individuals as well as lead and restore whole peoples. When people met Jesus they assumed he was a healer and would restore rather than condemn the sick and wounded. Condemn? Well, yes, because many people believed sickness was a punishment, an exclusion from God and the people of God. Even today, the sick will say: "Why is God punishing me?"

But in Jesus, the suffering of the sick is a special calling uniting their sickness to his dying on the cross. It is a final plunge, an anticipation of crossing the Jordan River, chilly and cold, and entering the Promised Land. Our sick need to be the focus of the parish's mission, but the sick also *have* a mission. There is a ministry to the sick and a ministry of the sick. We draw strength from those who are most closely united to the cross.

Teaching about sickness and healing

Healing is a great mystery, and the search for various ways to heal people suffering from all kinds of maladies remains central: The media makes a great deal of any kind of medical breakthrough. That there is a mind, spirit, body connection is now obvious to scientists. We must, though, make sure we do not give the impression that healing is "up to us" and that a failure to be healed is a sign of a weak will or shallow faith. Joyful trust in all circumstances is the key to understanding the sacrament.

You can begin by talking about sickness, when things happened that made the children sad, or fearful, or physically ill. Perhaps there was a relative or a friend, perhaps a time when they were sick themselves that can be shared without violating privacy.

Children, we know, are intimately involved in one very important aspect of this sacrament. Children often recover faster from serious illness than adults. They are naturally open to healing. This openness and trust is something that the children will be ready to share. You may be surprised at the things they will share with you while looking at a picture of Jesus healing someone. They will be happy to share with you what the sick person may be feeling, and you will be touched by what they say about Jesus healing people.

Teaching through the rite itself

The friend of the catechist here would be anyone of those seniors in the community who might agree to come and be anointed by the priest in front of the children. It is a beautiful and simple rite that communicates as it is celebrated. The interaction, the hugs, and the hand holding extended by the children to the seniors will give you, the children, and the seniors an idea of how sacraments express and foster community.

The sacrament takes place after a liturgy of the Word. It would be very helpful to take a large picture of Jesus showing compassion for the sick and place it where people can see it. This, along with the Word—some strong, simple gospel story about a healing—will make a powerful impression.

The sacrament itself has two parts: the laying on of hands and the anointing. There is a very important response, "Amen," from the one receiving the anointing. This sometimes gets lost. Catechists will do an important thing if they can really share how faith is increased when a Christian can say robustly, "Amen!" (Happy are the catechists who live in cultures where this is the norm!)

The laying on of hands in silence is the traditional way of communicating the Holy Spirit through the sacraments and through blessings. The sacred gesture should be a normal, regular experience. While not sacramental, something happens when the catechist blesses the children by putting her or his hands on their heads. Parents can do this with great effect as well.

Second, there is the anointing with oil. The anointing of the forehead has a prayer and a response: "Through this holy anointing may the Lord in his love and mercy help you with the grace of the Holy Spirit." The person anointed answers, "Amen!" Then the hands are anointed following the same pattern: "May the Lord who frees you from sin, save you and raise you." "Amen." The gesture of outstretched hands, the calling down of the Holy Spirit, and the call for the sick to be raised up all reflect back to baptism and Eucharist and confirmation.

Oil and lotions

I once was at a wonderful workshop where a master of spirituality poured out so many good things in such a short time, it seemed a miracle. But there was one moment, one lapse, and it produced a laugh.

The workshop took place in my home diocese of Honolulu. The leader, otherwise so wise, said he was stumped by the imagery of oil in the liturgy. Where, he asked, do people today anoint themselves or get themselves anointed by gobs of oil? I was startled, considering the location of the workshop, so I waited for a few seconds to see if someone else would chime in, but when they didn't, I blurted out the obvious: Waikiki! There was a big laugh because our leader had forgotten where he was. That famous beach in Honolulu is crowded with people slathered in all kinds of oils and sunscreens. The breeze mixes the smells very pleasantly but very strongly. The children we teach know a lot about all kinds of oils and lotions because we are very aware of the sun and our need for protection from ultraviolet rays. So the ancient custom of anointing is back in full force.

Reaching out

Parishes are discovering how helpful it is to have a parish nurse or even a parish social worker so that the healing ministry of Jesus can continue in a practical way. Catholic hospitals, clinics, and home nursing services will provide you with many resources to help you and the young people to see how compassion and healing are a constant call and joy.

The healing ministry of Jesus is an obvious part of the Good News message. You as a catechist will be able to keep the story going, the reality going, the blessings that come from this sacrament going in your community. The parish is always looking for ways to reach out to the sick and elderly. Your time of faith sharing will be a very important part of that ministry, and many creative ideas will flow out of your efforts, from the responses of the children and, especially, from your seniors, who will respond gladly to your invitations to share with the young people their experiences of illness and healing by the Holy Spirit sent by Jesus to your little local church.

FOR REFLECTION AND DISCUSSION

1. What do you think Jesus was experiencing when he encountered the sick? How did the sick respond to Jesus?

2. What different outward signs were chosen by Jesus for healing? Why so many different signs? What did these signs communicate?

3. How have you experienced illness? Have you been anointed? Have you ever been in the hospital? For many children, their only experience of the hospital is when their mom goes to have a baby. Be sure that the children you teach know the difference between going to the hospital to have a baby and going to the hospital for serious illness.

4. If you have an older person come to your session, the children will probably want to touch them. A little guidance on your part and preparation beforehand will be helpful. Seniors usually are grandparents and can handle children well. Children automatically respond to them. If the senior can answer questions about how illness has brought them to trust God more, they will do wonders for you and yours. You can think back yourself on your own suffering and share something of a healing that came out of that.

5. Olive oil is the basis for the anointing. Reflect on the wonder of oil coming not out of the ground, but from

olives growing on a tree. Seed to tree, tree to fruit, fruit to oil: another sign of transformation for you to meditate on. What other things change like that?

PRAYER

Loving Spirit of Jesus, you heal us when we suffer in mind and body. Your strength comes to us and turns our weakness into a time of trust. Help us to receive your healing and to offer your healing to others. Let the sick around us teach us patience and trust. Bless the suffering of your precious people and keep us close to Jesus, who is always with us. Amen.

Holy Orders

How does God lead us?

Moses was a prophet. Other prophets, real and fake, followed. Then there were anointed kings, some faithful, some mediocre, some disasters. There were priests. The Promised Land was ruined when the people set up another Egypt in the land of freedom that God had given them. So instead of a pharaoh, they had a king with taxes and injustice, armies and wars. The prophets, the true ones (not the ones hired by the king), tried to proclaim the mercy and justice of God and take a stand against all this evil.

So the Church has followed Jesus in being very careful about power. Jesus is a servant and so are the followers of Jesus. The compass for this sacrament always points—as the compasses for all the sacraments do—to the death and resurrection of Jesus.

There is a priesthood, but there is only one priest: Jesus Christ. All baptized Christians share in this priesthood, which is why we are able to offer ourselves with Christ when the Eucharist is celebrated. Through holy orders, the deacons, priests, and bishops also share in a different kind of priesthood so that they can promote the common priesthood of the baptized—the special gifts the Holy Spirit gives individuals and communities—and to provide the service of governance—how the pope and the bishops bring order and unity to this huge world Church and extend its ministry through the power to ordain priests and other bishops.

How to share this with young people?

Well, it sounds too cute to be true, but it is true: Children are told that the church building is God's house, and so a couple of times tots have come out from Mass and said to me, "Thanks, God" or "Thank you, Mr. God."

For sure, the young people see "the priest." Most have been through the sacrament of penance, and Sunday Mass remains a special if not exactly consistent experience. All the better if there is no cry room and if the children can see something of what is going on. A pro-life Church can get used to, and must get used to, welcoming children up front at Mass.

Up front, children see colored and white vestments, candles, and people moving around and up to the priest and back. At communion, the too-small ones get yanked past the priest or, to the consternation of some, get a little blessing. Older children display the same range of devotion or lack of it as the adults. If there is a lay minister instead of the priest, this does not seem to distract from the importance of the priest, who is usually in the middle in any case.

Despite scandal and abuse, a good number of young people still have a kind of affection for priests that seems to be no small miracle.

Now in many places, besides the priest there is a deacon. That deacon can be a married uncle, a dad, or a grandfather. Such a close relationship, such familiarity, adds a complicated, rich dimension to an essential ministry in the Church. In the Eastern Church, the deacon is more visible than the priest and more audible. The revered place for deacons and their wives is a major contribution from the East to us raised in the "Western Church."

Bishops, priests, deacons

The local Church hangs together, is "ordered," through holy orders. There is first and always the bishop with the pope being the bishop of Rome. This is very clear at a liturgy where the bishop presides. It is also very clear that the deacon at such a liturgy is very important. For many years I was blessed with two deacons who took turns ministering at daily Mass. One parishioner actually complained that I did nothing for most of the first part of the Mass! Indeed, that was a good observation. Priests became necessary when the bishop could not get around to the churches. Deacons were there from the beginning, or nearly so.

When the deacon is ordained, the bishop presents him with the Gospel Book and then says: "Receive the Gospel of Christ, whose herald you have become. Believe what you read, teach what you believe, and practice what you teach." These words capture the great foundation of ministry.

The deacon is a servant. That's what the word "deacon" means. The priest is also like Christ, who is among us as one who serves. The bishop, the pastor of everyone in the local church, has the incredible responsibility of shepherding a large and complex local church, being faithful to it, and keeping it in communion with the whole Church, with the other bishops and the pope. Even the pope is a servant: a servant of the servants of God. The service of unity in the Church keeps the pope as humble as Peter the Apostle, who had the first responsibility of uniting and strengthening the Church.

Your young people will not see much of the pope or the bishop. Numbers just make that nearly impossible. But they will see and hear the local priests and deacons. And the occasional visit of the bishop or even the pope will bring some excitement.

Connecting children to the bishops, priests, and deacons

Catechists today can help tremendously by inviting the deacon and his family into the sessions concerning holy orders. The young people could send birthday cards to the deacons and priests. Get-well cards sent when the priest, deacon, or bishop is sick is a task that belongs to the whole community, but especially to catechists and those they teach.

You will have two tasks: to share your faith about the ministry of the bishop, priests, and deacons and at the same time to communicate that those in holy orders are human beings too. There are tremendous pressures on those in these ministries. Sometimes we have to shepherd the shepherds. Those in holy orders serve knowing that the Holy Spirit gives special gifts to some in the larger community and that this ministry enhances holy orders and does not distract from them. Popes have made women, who are excluded from holy orders, "doctors of the church." That means that even popes can learn from the larger community. Someone like St. Catherine of Siena, a laywoman, rather insisted that the pope listen to her. And so he did.

Good pastoring takes good listening, and the good priests and deacons will go out of their way to listen to you and the special experience you bring to the Church. When the Second Vatican Council was called in the early 1960s, our bishop asked everyone—at the request of Pope John XXIII—to send in suggestions for the Council. So I, a sophomore in high school, wrote the bishop with my suggestion that the Mass be celebrated in the vernacular, or failing that, at least in audible Latin. (The Latin Low Mass was silent except for what the servers could hear.) And the bishop wrote me back thanking me for the suggestion. He was, as a matter of fact, dead set against liturgical changes, but he did take the time to register my two cents.

FOR REFLECTION AND DISCUSSION

1. Bishops ordain deacons and priests. They also ordain priests to be bishops. Have you been to any of these ordinations? How might you share the joy and hope that seems spontaneous at these ordinations?

2. A visit in the parish church where penance is celebrated and baptisms take place will put the minister of these sacraments in focus. What do you feel when you see the priest and deacons faithfully fulfilling their ministry of sacramental life? Do you have any relatives or friends that are in holy orders? What has that meant to you?

3. There are plenty of storybooks, short films, and, for older children, feature films about heroic priests, deacons, and bishops. Keeping these available and being familiar with them helps everyone appreciate the heroic lives of some of our Church leaders.

4. If you know a priest's family or a bishop's family, you might invite them to the parish to share stories. They may have some family photos that will remind you where it all started.

5. Visiting a seminary is not always possible, but having someone from the seminary come over can be arranged. The more familiarity your students develop with persons in, or preparing to enter, holy orders, the more they can appreciate this sacrament.

PRAYER

God, you call all your people to service and bless us, your Church, with the special ministries that give us life as followers of Jesus. When we gather for the sacraments, when we hear your Word, help us to pray that our bishops, priests, and deacons will shine with the gifts of the Holy Spirit and enrich the whole Church and the world with their ministry. Amen.

Marriage

If there is an image for heaven, for the Promised Land, for the goal that Jesus leads us toward, it is marriage. Slavery was the ultimate destruction of love and the human person because slaves had no right to a family or to their own children. What kind of hope can a slave have? So the Promised Land where Moses led the people was a land where love and hard work gave people hope, where marriage and a future were possible. What a blessing not only to see our children but our children's children! So, of course, marriage is a holy thing and is the most prevalent, even if arduous, path to the eternal wedding banquet promised us by God.

Who ministers the sacrament?

Baptism unites all Christians. All Catholics are baptized, and, as we have seen, baptizing may be done by anyone with the right intention. A priest is not essential to the sacrament of baptism. The priest also does not administer the sacrament of marriage. So two sacraments Catholics receive—baptism and marriage—do not by necessity involve clergy.

In marriage it is the couple themselves who give each other the sacrament. The priest or deacon required by the Church is there as a witness not as a sacramental minister. It should puzzle people to hear a priest say he "married" a couple or to hear a couple say something like "Father Smith married us!" He most certainly did not! What the priest or deacon witnesses is captured very well in the words that can be chosen from the liturgy book: The man says, "I take you to be my wife. I promise to be true to you in good times and in bad, in sickness and in health. I will love you and honor you all the days of my life." The woman vows the same. Both, of course, use their names and the names of their spouse as part of the vow. The name given at baptism now is the name given and received in the sacrament of matrimony.

If there were no priest or deacon to witness the marriage, the man and woman could—for instance, on a desert island—scratch their consent on a rock or coconut. Some kind of public witness attests that they did marry each other.

The core expression

Jesus loved weddings. Jesus had several images of heaven, but the most consistent one describes eternal life as a marriage banquet—a Mediterranean-style marriage banquet—not a polite, legal justice of the peace marriage or an austere, puritanical ceremony barely conceding the necessity of sexual love. Sexual love and, by extension, the marvelous gift of children, if granted, is a core expression of the sacrament.

In the Old Testament, the secular and sexual love poem called the "Song of Songs" has, without too many people apologizing for it, given us an understanding of how God makes most people holy in the sexuality that is central to human creation. In that wonderful book of the Bible a coy lover hears her lover at the door and says, "I am naked, you cannot come in." This is nonsense so the lover keeps knocking. "I cannot get out of bed to let you in. I will get my feet dirty." This is more nonsense but the lover goes away and the rest of the poem is about sanity and love finally being regained in the pursuit of the lover, who promises that love is stronger than death. I told this synopsis to my little congregation of southern Catholics— Bible readers at that—and some thought I was making it up! They could not believe that is in the Bible! Well, it is.

If you are married, you are your own great source for faith sharing. You also get a chance to talk about forgiveness, fair fighting, sharing, and giving the other person a break. These are things the children may or may not experience in their own families.

Be sensitive

As a catechist, you need to be very sensitive about the young ones who come from divorced families or who know divorcing couples. While the culture tries to help by making romance very spectacular, marriage, like religion, thrives really on the routine of love that moves past disillusion and hurt. You can talk about marriage by talking about friendship. Everyone has had to forgive a friend. Everyone knows how tough family life can be.

But young people, for all the traditional rebellion they engage in, know their safety lies in having a family to rebel against. The splitting up of a family carries devastation with it. It is not fashionable to talk about this, but you must be sensitive to the fact that divorce often makes the children assume the role of responsible adults while their separating mother and father regress. This is laying too heavy a burden on them, and catechists could help them considerably here. You will have, as a catechist, the challenge of upholding marriage as a sacrament while being compassionate to the real situations the young people face. Here above all, knowing your little community is very important.

In any case there are plenty of funny as well as tender stories that will help you get away from the unrealistic, romantic ideas that still prevail. Humor and tenderness mark this sacrament of real Christian living and should naturally keep the interest of any young person who will come to believe that heaven is like a wedding banquet.

FOR REFLECTION AND DISCUSSION

1. Sometimes people will forget that everyone, single people included, have families—nobody was hatched! So being single should not exclude some real personal reflection about the sacrament of marriage. How has family spoken of God's love for you? Who are the most surprising and creative people in your family? Your reflections shared in a heartfelt way will make a profound impact on the young people in your charge.

2. Mothers telling children stories about their faith, especially at Christmas and Easter time, have a major influence on the faith life of the young. Maybe you know one of these women who are especially good at the stories. She could tell you the story or come to your sessions with the children.

3. There are not many pictures of married saints. You could have fun on the Internet finding them. They don't have to be canonized. Grandparents in the parish are wonderful gifts, and the children might want to meet some people married for 50 years.

4. If your parents had a happy marriage, perhaps you could bring in family pictures. The young will be especially happy to see them.

5. Separated, widowed, and divorced parents are a significant part of the parish. Be on the lookout among your young people and be prepared to support them if their family life is suffering. Ask your parish and diocesan resource people for help here.

6. The music used to celebrate weddings has traditionally canceled out the substance of the wedding. A popular recessional from the Richard Wagner opera, Lohengrin, is a march to the bridal chamber where the brother-in-law is killed by the groom and the bride dies from grief. Somehow that made it into the liturgy as a recessional. That has changed some: Now we have music from the movie *Titanic*! You might want to do some music education here.

PRAYER

Dear God of us all, make us a real family in our parish. Bless our mothers and fathers. Help us to look out for each other. Help us to be ready to forgive each other. Help us to keep growing in love, in faith, and in hope. Amen.

Conclusion

Decades of preparing people for sacraments never dull the one responsible for the sharing. The sacrament is Jesus, and Jesus is always new and exciting. The Church shares in this life of Christ among us. The sacraments express this reality, foster this reality, and prepare us all for the fulfillment of the reality after death when we see God face to face. Seeds planted in the ground gradually are transformed into something that would be unimaginable even if the seed could think! It is the same with us. We are transformed. Our eyes have not seen, nor our ears heard, what God has prepared for us. Nor has it entered into our hearts because we are on this side of the reality where faith is given us, and shared by you the family, by you the catechist, by you the parish, by you the priest, by you the deacon, by you the bishop, and celebrated as sacraments: sacraments in the Christ who leads us from life here and now to everlasting life—the resurrection and transformation—where hope is fulfilled and the journey ends in the everlasting arms of God.

The Unicorn Sonata

The Unicorn Sonata

Peter S. Beagle

Author of *The Last Unicorn*

Illustrations by Robert Rodriguez

Turner Publishing, Inc.

ATLANTA

Copyright © 1996 by Peter S. Beagle.

Illustrations copyright © 1996 by Robert Rodriguez.

All rights reserved under international copyright conventions. No part of the contents of this book may be reproduced or utilized in any form or by any means, electronic or mechanical, including photocopying, recording, or by any information storage and retrieval system, without the written consent of the publisher.

PUBLISHED BY TURNER PUBLISHING, INC.
A SUBSIDIARY OF TURNER BROADCASTING SYSTEM, INC.
1050 TECHWOOD DRIVE, N. W.
ATLANTA, GEORGIA 30318
DISTRIBUTED BY ANDREWS AND MCMEEL
A UNIVERSAL PRESS SYNDICATE COMPANY
4900 MAIN STREET
KANSAS CITY, MISSOURI 64112

10 9 8 7 6 5 4 3 2 1

PRINTED IN THE U.S.A.

For Joseph H. Mazo

I miss you, Yossele.

Acknowledgments

Without Janet Berliner, The Unicorn Sonata would not exist.
Without Stephen Roxburgh, it wouldn't be the book it is.

Janet Berliner didn't write The Unicorn Sonata, but that's about the only
thing she didn't do, from the very beginning and even before that.
The tale wouldn't have occurred to me independently: It was Janet
who called out of nowhere, Janet who brought up the whole utterly
impossible proposition, Janet who had me on a plane to Atlanta
and Turner Publishing within a week.
She's always doing that.

It was Janet who hashed out the original plot with me, Janet—along with
her road manager and rhythm section, the legendary "Cowboy Bob"
Fleck—who was always an area code away to call on for help and highly
specific suggestions whenever the story did an unexpected backflip or hair-
pin turn, as stories will. Even after the tale was off the ground and flying on
its own, Janet was unceasingly there to keep it in contact with the earth.
She combines the soul of at least two poets,
with the intense practicality of a Nebraska farmer.
You can't do better than that.

No Janet Berliner, no Unicorn Sonata. Like that. Just so it's clear.

Stephen Roxburgh is an absolute anachronism, a throwback to the oldtime
editors who I was lucky enough to encounter when I was young. I didn't
know enough to appreciate them then, those patient, stubborn,
aggravating souls who cared enough about words and thoughts and
imaginary people to argue about them all night; those people for whom
books weren't "product" or "properties," but living individual creations in
which texture is everything. Stephen's the first one of those I've met in
a very long time. I hope he knows how grateful I am.

The Unicorn Sonata

Chapter One

It seemed to her that the street went on forever. Late spring had turned breathlessly hot, and Joey's bookbag banged the sticky place between her shoulders as she trudged past gas stations, parking lots, beauty salons, Rent-to-Owns, mini-malls full of video stores, karate schools, health-food markets, and multiplex movie theatres—all repeating themselves every few blocks, unchanging as the small tune that Joey whistled over and over. There were no trees, and no grass. There was no horizon.

Near one corner, a tiny Greek restaurant barely separated a real-estate office and a shoe outlet. Joey stood in the doorway for a moment, looking quickly from table to table, then turned away and moved on another half-block to a window full of guitars, trumpets, and violins. The faded golden lettering said: PAPAS MUSIC—SALES & REPAIRS. Joey squinted at her reflection, made a face at the angular thirteen-year-old image that looked back at her, straightened her hair, tugged hard on the heavy door, and walked in.

AFTER THE HARD SUNLIGHT OF THE STREET, the little shop felt as dim and cool as swimming underwater at summer camp. It smelled of fresh sawdust, of old felt, of metal and wood polish.

Joey promptly sneezed. The gray-haired man fitting a new reed into a saxophone said without looking up, "Miss Josephine Angelina Rivera. Still allergic to music."

"I'm allergic to *dust*," Joey said loudly. She unslung her backpack and plopped it down on the floor. "If you'd vacuum this dump just every couple of years—"

The man snorted explosively. "So we're in a good mood today, a mean mood?" His hoarse voice had a quality that was not quite an accent—it was more like an echo of another language, half forgotten. "Newspaper, they ought to print a Rivera forecast every morning, like the weather." John Papas was sixty or sixty-five, short and thickset, triangular dark eyes somber above high cheekbones, a broad, powerful nose, and a shaggy gray-black mustache. He put the saxophone back in its case. "Your people know you're here? The truth, now."

Joey nodded. John Papas snorted again. "Sure they do. Some day I call your mother, find out she knows how much time you spend in this dump, maybe she won't like it so much. I got enough troubles, who needs trouble with your family? You give me your phone number, I just give them a call, hah?"

"Yeah, well, call real late," Joey mumbled. "They're not exactly in a whole lot." She straddled a chair, put her head down on the backrest, and closed her eyes.

John Papas picked up a battered clarinet, apparently studying the valves intently before he spoke again. "So. How'd it go, the big science test?"

Joey shrugged without raising her head. "Terrible. Like I

figured." John Papas ran a scale, growled irritably, and tried the same run in a lower key. Joey said, "I can't do anything right. Nothing. You name it, I screw it up. Tests, homework, gym class—I'm going to fail *volleyball*, for God's sake. My twitty little brother's doing better in school than I am." She pounded the back of the chair, opened her eyes and added, "Dances better, too. And better-looking."

"You help me good around here," John Papas said. Joey looked away. "You make up music. Let's see your gym teacher, your handsome brother do that." When she did not answer, John Papas asked, "So tell me. We come for lesson, for hang around and brood, for be some practical use to an old man. Which?"

Joey's thoughts drifted back from a very long way off. She looked away, muttering, "Everything, I guess."

"Everything," John Papas repeated. "Okay, very fine. *I* go now to Provotakis's dump, buy myself whatever he's calling lunch this week. Maybe play a little chess, he's not too busy cheating his cash register. *You*, you sweep up, vacuum, whatever you like, see can you maybe fix the toilet one more time." He grinned at her then, briefly and warmly. "I get back, we talk a little music, do some more with the chords, maybe we even try writing some of your things down this time. The brooding we worry about later. Good deal?"

Joey nodded. John Papas started briskly for the door, adding over his shoulder, "Remember, the grabby little hands, they stay out of my stuff. The guy, what's his name, comes in for his sax, tell him wait. I be back quick, bring you some good Greek coffee."

When he had gone, Joey looked around her with a suddenly proprietary eye. The shop was one large room divided into two

13

small ones only by mood. The side where she stood was the showroom, crowded with instrument display cases, music racks, and the shadows of the guitars hanging on the walls. The far side, darker and more orderly, served as John Papas's workroom-office combination. These walls were whitewashed and bare, except for two framed concert posters in Greek. A few stringed instruments and far more reeds and woodwinds were carefully laid out on a long table in various states of disassembly, with numbered tags attached to them. A tall metal chest in a shadowy corner held John Papas's tools.

Joey sneezed again and got to work. She spent most of her time in the showroom, putting music books and brochures back in their racks, picking up countless styrofoam coffee cups, and emptying the two ashtrays spilling thin black cigar butts across a drift of bills and receipts on the counter. She hummed a notably different melody now than she had on the streets, her face relaxing slowly as she tidied. In a voice that was slightly higher and a good deal clearer than her speaking voice, she scat-sang wordlessly to herself, almost unaware. The tune wandered raggedly between minor and major, changing key apparently at random. Joey thought of it as her dishwashing song, when she thought about it at all.

She fixed the leaking toilet, reminding herself to remind John Papas once again to replace the ancient flap-and-ball assembly, and went to the broom closet for the vacuum cleaner, singing loudly enough now to hear herself over the rattling howl. She cleaned patiently and assiduously, even vacuuming the back stairs, which led out to a parking lot. Because of the machine's racket, she didn't hear the shop door open; when she shut off the vacuum cleaner and turned to see the boy, she let out a gasp of surprise that sounded like a scream in the sudden quiet.

The boy smiled at her, holding up both hands with the palms outward. "I will not hurt you," he said. "I am Indigo."

He was slightly made, hardly taller than Joey herself, and looking no older; but there was a fluidity to his movements that made her think of television documentaries about leopards and cheetahs. He wore a blue windbreaker, zipped up even in the Valley heat, drab chino pants, and dilapidated running shoes; and his eyes were the darkest blue she had ever seen—true indigo—set in a heart-shaped face whose skin looked almost transparent. He had a wide mouth, and small, pointed ears—not like Mr. Spock's on television, but definitely pointed all the same. Joey thought he was the most beautiful person she had ever seen, and she was afraid of him.

"I am Indigo," the boy said again. "I am looking for—" and he fumbled strangely for words—"Papas Music. This is Papas Music?" His accent was different from John Papas's, more rhythmically cadenced, like the voices of the West Indian girls in her school.

"This is Papas Music," Joey said, "but Mr. Papas isn't here right now. He'll be back in just a little. Can *I* help you?"

Indigo smiled again. Joey noticed that his eyes got darker and more secret when he smiled. He did not answer her but reached inside his windbreaker and drew out a horn. It was as long as his forearm, spiraled as a seashell, and at first Joey thought it was plastic, because of the color, which was the kind of deep, shimmering silver-blue that you got in giveaway makeup kits, and in models of sports cars. But when he put the horn to his lips Joey realized with the first notes that it was made of no material she knew. The tone was soft, but warm and rich, sounding neither like wood nor brass—it might have been a distant human voice, singing without words of a place it knew

15

that she didn't. Hearing it made her throat lock up and her eyes sting; and yet she was amazed to feel herself smiling.

There were no fingerstops; nothing but the one flattened hole at the horn's tip to blow into. The notes sounded random at first, but then they flowed together into a slow-swaying, silver-blue air whose rhythm kept eluding her, slipping constantly out of reach like a playful kitten. Joey stood, forgetting entirely where she was, only her head moving slightly as Indigo played. He never moved, but the music itself drew nearer, a kitten gaining courage: one moment as comfortingly familiar as a nursery rhyme; then, in the next, as cold and foreign as moonlight turned into melody. Once or twice she put her hand out hesitantly, as though to stroke the sounds, but each time the boy's look became so fiercely wary that she drew her hand back. It seemed to her that the horn was glowing steadily brighter as he played on, and that if she followed the blue-and-silver spirals with her gaze, very carefully, they would lead her all the way around and down, into the music. Indigo watched her, his eyes expressionless now, the deep blue gone the deeper black of interstellar space on *Star Trek*.

Joey had no idea how long he had been playing, nor how long John Papas had been standing in the doorway. She turned only when she heard the gentle rasp demanding, "So excuse me? Who we have here?" Indigo immediately stopped playing and whirled to face him, bowing over the horn.

"He was looking for you," Joey said. Her voice sounded strange and loud to her after the music. "His name is Indigo."

"Indigo," John Papas said. "Your parents went to Woodstock, huh?" The joke came out in a strange, expressionless undertone. He was staring at the boy in what was clearly recognition, his face colorless, his eyes a little too wide. In the same flat voice, John Papas asked, "What is that? Show me."

Indigo bowed again and offered him the silver-blue horn. John Papas took it slowly, still looking at the boy as he ran his hands over it, plainly surprised to find no stops. He brought the horn to his mouth and blew across the hole, then into it, lightly at first, puffing and tonguing harder when no sound came out. Finally—red-faced now, and understandably irritated—he said, "So. Do it again."

Smiling still, Indigo took the horn back. "It is not for everyone, I think." Tilting the horn so that it pointed toward the old-fashioned transom window over the shop door, he began to play a tune as simple as a blackbird's call, so sweetly unpretentious that it frightened Joey in a way she could never have imagined. The hair prickled on her neck, her lips and cheeks grew painfully stiff, and her stomach cramped coldly. But the music danced on, surging out of Indigo through the horn without any need of fingers to shape or guide it: a child's tin whistle one moment, then a distant voice again, a voice that halfway mocked its own music, tempting and taunting at the same time.

Next to Joey, John Papas was breathing like a runner, his mouth slack, his head moving with the music. When it ended he said, low and harsh, "What is that thing? Where did you get it?"

"It is mine," Indigo said. "It comes from very far away."

John Papas said, "Synthetic, has to be. There's nothing in nature makes a sound like that. This is my business, boy, I know."

Without answering, Indigo made as though to put the horn back under his windbreaker. At this John Papas gave a small, hoarse gasp, as though he had been hit in the stomach. In the nearly six months since she first wandered into his shop, Joey had never heard him utter such a sound, nor seen anything like the raw longing in his face. He said softly, "What do you want for it?" Reaching out to take the silver-blue horn again, he dropped a cardboard cup, and Joey realized too late that he had kept his promise to bring her coffee. It splashed near her on the floor, stinging her ankles, but she did not move.

John Papas shook his head hard, clearly trying to wake himself from a clinging dream. He said slowly, his Greek accent more noticeable than usual, "I will buy. Tell me what you want."

Indigo hesitated, seeming off balance himself for the first time. "It will cost you very much, Mr. Papas."

John Papas moistened his lips. He said, "I'm waiting." Indigo continued to look uncertain, even anxious, and John Papas said, more strongly, "Come on, come on, what are you asking? How much?"

"Gold," the boy said. "I want gold." John Papas stared at him, and so did Joey. Indigo backed away a little, his grip on the horn tightening. He said, "In my—my country, there is no such thing as money, no buying or selling for bits of paper as you do here. But I travel much, and I see how everyone always wants gold, everywhere. You must pay me in gold."

Joey laughed outright. "Mr. Papas doesn't have any gold— what do you think he is, a pirate?" Indigo turned toward her, and she took a step backward. "Nobody has gold anymore," she said. "That's in books, for God's sake."

But John Papas put a hand back to quiet her, saying harshly, "Wait, be quiet, girl," and then to Indigo, "So. How much gold?"

Indigo's smile and cool assurance returned almost instantly. "How much have you?" John Papas opened his mouth and closed it again. Indigo said, "If gold is rare, the horn is rarer. Believe me."

John Papas stood looking at him for a long time before he

nodded. He said, "Wait," then turned and went away into the darkness of the workroom. Joey heard the door of the tiny corner cubicle that served as his office open and close. Stranded with Indigo, as though left to entertain some tedious relative, she looked past him, not quite meeting his disquieting eyes. Through the storefront window she could see the flat, hot street outside, with cars grinding by and odd occasional figures swirling up close, then growing small again, like fish circling in a bowl. In the light of Indigo's sideways smile, the drearily familiar world outside the window began to seem as unreal as the world into which her father and mother vanished every day. She was grateful to hear John Papas returning.

"Gold," he said. "You want gold, boy? Papas will show you gold." He was carrying a wooden box under one arm. It was long and shallow, looking like a painter's portfolio, even to the stains and splotches on the sides. When John Papas set it down on the counter, Joey heard a hard, sliding rattle inside, and she felt her breath scrape the back of her throat. John Papas fitted a double-faced key into a place where there didn't seem to be a keyhole. The lock made no sound when he turned it. John Papas threw back the lid, and Joey saw that the box was half-full of old coins, each between a dime and a silver dollar in size. Some had raised patterns and designs on their surfaces, while others were worn as smooth as marbles, but all were the dirty yellow-brown shade of the box's brass fittings. They smelled faintly dank, although they were quite dry; they smelled of earth.

"Drachmas," John Papas said. "Guineas, crowns, sovereigns, half-eagles. You got ducats, doubloons, like in the pirate books you got *moidores*, God's sake. For the horn, even up." His lips were tight and pale, slightly baring his teeth.

When he saw Joey looking at him, he said harshly, "Not mine, Josephine Rivera. My father's. *His* father's, part of it. We are Greek. Greek means you never know when you might have to get out fast. Buy a passport, a visa, bribe yourself a captain, a cop, a border guard. Nobody will help you, never, never, only gold. Only gold." He shook the box violently, and the coins hissed heavily against each other.

Indigo picked up a few of the coins and turned them over on his palm, shoving them this way and that. John Papas said, "My father, he gave this to me when he died. Until now, I have not sold one. Not one, a Greek might need sometime. Now, for that horn, all. *Take*, boy!" He pushed the box hard at Indigo's face.

The boy looked from him to Joey, then back again. He glanced at the coins with casual curiosity, but it seemed to Joey that his earlier anxiety was again turning fathoms deep in the dark-blue eyes. Looking straight at Joey, he scooped up a larger handful of the coins, wrinkling his forehead.

"Take," John Papas repeated impatiently. "Go ahead, every one is genuine, you get a good price from any dealer, better from a collector. Here." He shoved the box hard into the boy's hands and reached for the silver-blue horn.

"No," Indigo said abruptly. "No, it is not enough." He turned suddenly and put the horn into Joey's hand. Their fingers touched for an instant, and Joey felt a soft, hot shiver in her bones. Indigo said, "Play. Show him why it is not enough."

The horn smelled of faraway flowers. As soon as it touched Joey's lips, she and it were one, feeling and making the music together, with no partition at all between them. She was not conscious even of blowing into it, nor of trying to shape sound into melody—the music was simply there, and had always been there, dancing through her on its way. *And something else was there, too,* something that was all around her, welcoming and frightening at once, something she would see immediately if she opened her eyes. But they had been shut since she began to play, and she kept them shut now, because there was some part of her that was blindly afraid.

A long way off, Indigo's voice said, "Stop now." Joey always wondered afterward whether she could have stopped playing—or being played—if he had not spoken. She put the horn down on the counter with shaking hands and opened her eyes. John Papas was staring at her with a look that mingled terror and absolute joy, and the strange boy was smiling, picking up the silver-blue horn.

"My name is Indigo," he said. "Remember me, Papas Music. Perhaps I will come here again."

With that he was gone, as completely as he had been present when Joey turned from vacuuming the back stairs. She opened the shop door very slowly and blinked out into the world she knew, but there was no sign of him anywhere. Behind her, John Papas said gently, "Close it. Close it, Josephine."

Joey shut the door and leaned against it. John Papas was standing by the counter, mopping his forehead. He looked more like himself than he had since Indigo walked into the shop, but he also looked older, Joey thought, and very tired. He shuffled his hand aimlessly through the box of old coins, not looking at them.

"Did you know him from somewhere?" Joey asked. John Papas looked up swiftly. "What, him? You think I go around knowing people named Indigo, Cadmium Yellow, whatever? You think I'm someone would know someone like that boy? Forget it. Never saw him in my life." He was too angry; it fit him poorly. Joey said, "Well, it just looked like it. And you looked like you knew that music, too." She felt tired and irritable and strange.

John Papas stared at her for what seemed like a very long time, his eyes empty of everything but her reflection. Joey stared back, stubbornly refusing to blink. John Papas scratched his head and began to smile slowly, a one-sided smile, as though a hook were set in his lip. He said, "Josephine Rivera." Then he said something in another language; and then, in English, "Josephine Rivera, where you ever come from? Where you come from, hanging around with an old Greek in a dusty old music shop? Why ain't you out playing baseball, football, out with your boyfriend, go dancing? Go to the movies?" He was still fighting the smile, but it was invading his eyes anyway.

"I don't like baseball," Joey said. "And I don't have a boyfriend, and I dance all wrong, everybody says so. I *like* being here, helping out and whatever. I just wish you'd tell me what's going on. What's wrong with me asking that?"

John Papas sighed. "What's wrong is, I'm not used to it, that kind of talk don't got to do with music, with fixing up instruments. You live alone like me, you forget how people talk." He worried at his mustache, tugging first one end and then the other, then smoothing both sides with his knuckles. He said finally, "Josephine Rivera, you ever get the feeling like something walks along right beside you—turn your head just a little, *there* it is? Only when you turn your head, nothing? You ever feel like that?"

Joey nodded. "Like when you know somebody's looking at you, but you can't see them?"

"Like that," John Papas agreed. "Also maybe like you're the one looking at something, it's right there, right across the street maybe, except you see only a little piece of it, you never can see the whole thing. That happens to you sometimes?"

"I think so," Joey said slowly. "My Abuelita, my grandmother, when I was really little she used to tell me if I turned my head fast enough I could look in my own ear. Sort of like that, in a way."

John Papas suddenly looked tired and vague. "Yah," he said. "Well, you keep your eyes open, that's all." He rubbed his mustache again, tucked the coin box under one arm, and turned back toward his shadowy workroom.

Joey said, "That boy. Indigo."

John Papas halted with his back to her. "Nothing to tell. Go home, I'm closing early, I just feel like it. Goodbye."

"Okay," Joey said. "Goodbye." Her voice came out sounding small and hurt, and she was furious with herself for it. She took a step after him, beginning to ask, "You want me to come in tomorrow?" and halted, because the music was there again . . .

. . . *faraway now, somehow as much in time as in distance, a sound with a smell to it, a green and dark smell, and apples, and great feathers warm in sunshine. The melody soars and demands, then drops away downwind like a kite; now as close as my own breathing, now so distant I have to listen with my skin, not my ears. Where is it, where is it? I have to go there.*

She had not realized that she had whispered the last words until she heard John Papas's voice. "Where is what? What are you talking about?"

"The music," Joey said. "That same music, where's it coming from?" John Papas stared at her. Joey said, "*There*, now, right there." She looked around wildly, then ran to the door again, crying out, "Where's it coming from? It's everywhere, can't you hear it?" The door stuck shut, as it always did, and she hurt her wrist and broke a fingernail shoving at it, trying to get to the music.

Then John Papas was beside her, one hand gently on her shoulder. The music faded, though she could still feel it in the hairs on her forearms and taste it on her dry lips. John Papas said quietly, "Go home, Josephine Rivera. You go straight on home, don't stop for nothing, don't *listen* to nothing. Plug in your Walkman, listen to that. We talk more later, tomorrow maybe. Here, here, your books. Go home now."

"It's that boy," Joey said. "Indigo. The music started with him. Mr. Papas, I have to know—"

"Tomorrow," John Papas said. "Maybe. Home now." He pushed the door open, shooed Joey through it, and was already pulling down the narrow shade and turning the cardboard sign to read CLOSED as she slung the bookbag back on her shoulders.

Chapter Two

*I*t was the first of the month, so Abuelita was there for dinner. They ate later than usual, because Mr. Rivera had had to detour all the way around to the Silver Pines Guest and Rest Home after work to pick up Abuelita. She sat across from Joey at the table: small and brown and perfectly round, her smooth black hair thinner now, but as shiny as ever. Each time she caught Joey looking at her, Abuelita's smile was as slow and complete as sunrise.

Joey was never sure how old her grandmother really was— her father always said Abuelita didn't know herself—and from childhood she had had real trouble imagining her as her father's mother. It wasn't for lack of resemblance, because Mr. Rivera had black hair and stubby fingers and small, delicate ears like Abuelita; it was rather that nothing capricious and unknown ever looked out of his eyes, no swift, secret mischief ever shared itself only with her. Very young, Joey had been plagued by an anxiety that Abuelita did not really belong to her family, but had merely adopted them for her own mysterious reasons, and might vanish back to her true children and grandchildren any time she chose. Even now she still dreamed about it.

In loud Coahuila Spanish, Abuelita asked Joey's ten-year-old brother Scott, sitting next to her, how he was doing at school. He squirmed in his chair, pushing his food around the plate and looking at his father. Mr. Rivera answered for him in English. "He's getting really good grades, Mama. He's in a special gifted class, and he plays soccer, too. His team might go to the state finals this year."

"But he can't speak Spanish," Abuelita said. "My grandson can't speak to me in our language." There was nothing angry or accusing or even regretful in her tone—it was only unusual in its lack of humor—but Mr. Rivera's face flushed anyway.

Joey's mother intervened. "Mama, he doesn't have the time, he's so busy with school and the team, and his friends and all. And he doesn't—you know—he just doesn't *hear* Spanish very much."

"Not in this neighborhood," Abuelita agreed pleasantly. "But 'Fina speaks as well as I do." No one but Abuelita ever called Joey by the childhood name.

"Well, you were living with us then," Mrs. Rivera said. "Before we moved. The circumstances were different."

Abuelita nodded. "*Muy diferente, las circunstancias.*" She turned back to Scott and patted his hand, speaking to him in English as carefully as though he were the foreigner. "Do you know what *I* think? *I* think you and I ought to take a trip down to Las Perlas this summer. When your school is over, just the two of us. A couple of months in Las Perlas, you will be speaking like a proper *coahuileño*. Maybe even develop a taste for *menudo*, who knows?" She winked at Joey.

Scott rose to the bait, as he always did. "*Menudo* is *gross*! A cow's stomach lining—barf, barf, *ralph*!" He doubled over his plate, and for a moment Joey thought that he really might be about to throw up. He could do it on command—or, more practically, on a bet. Abuelita looked sideways at him, and he sat up straight.

"Gilberto?" she asked Mr. Rivera. "What do you think? Maybe we could all go to Las Perlas. The children should see where they are from, where we began. I would like us to go to Las Perlas."

The quick *let-me-handle-this* glance her father shot at his wife was as familiar to Joey as the change in his voice when the phone call was someone from work. He said, "Well, Mama, I'm not sure Las Perlas even exists anymore. I think they probably just paved it over. Years back."

"Las Perlas is there," Abuelita answered quietly. "Las Perlas exists."

"I don't want to go there," Scott said. "Coach is taking the whole team to Disneyland if we get to the finals."

Joey sat in back with Abuelita when Mr. Rivera drove her back to Silver Pines. They held hands. Joey said, "Look, I'm not doing anything special this summer. I'll go with you to Las Perlas, if you want."

Abuelita shook her head. "I am thinking too much about Las Perlas these days, 'Fina. Not a good thing in an old woman. We will just forget about it."

Joey squeezed her hand. "Okay, we'll go the way we used to go to China, remember? When I was little, in the old house? Sit in the backyard and dig. We could still do that."

Abuelita had one particular smile that always made her look to Joey like the tiny, naughty black-eyed girl she must have been, long ago, running barefoot down a muddy street after a goat. "*Ay*, that magic backyard. We went to Oaxaca there, didn't we? And India. I remember, 'Fina."

"The yard wasn't magic," Joey said. "You were. You still are."

She hugged Abuelita goodbye on the graveled driveway of Silver Pines, saying, "I'll see you Sunday, same time as always. Anything you want me to bring?"

"Bring me a song," Abuelita said. "One of those songs you make up, I would like that. You could sing it to me when we take our walk."

"Deal," Joey said. She got back into the car quickly, because she always hated to watch Abuelita trudge across the courtyard, dwindling and disappearing in the dazzle of the lighted fountain. She said to her father, "Every time we drop her off like this, I think, *What if it's the last time, just suppose?* I can't help it, I always think that."

Mr. Rivera answered, "Mama's tough as nails. She'll outlive us all, believe me." For the rest of the way home he was dictating notes to himself on his pocket recorder, so Joey curled against the door and thought about digging to China and India with Abuelita.

She had trouble falling asleep that night, finally managing a fretful doze from which she woke some hours later to a dark, still house with the dishwasher still growling. She slipped down to the kitchen for a glass of chocolate milk, and sprawled back on her bed with one of her mother's romance novels, waiting patiently to get sleepy.

Well past midnight, still wide awake, she was just beginning to wonder whether there was a chance of getting away with watching TV if she lay on the floor in front of it and played it really, *really* softly, when she heard the music, so close that before she recognized it she thought that Scott must have fallen asleep with his damn stupid radio on again. But it was outside, right outside, calling in the street, and Joey had two locks and a deadbolt undone before she realized that the music had stopped. She heard herself cry out in sorrow, but no one woke.

She went out onto the front step and stood listening. No sound now but the hiccuppy hiss of the lawn sprinklers coming on, and the mumble of freeway traffic in the distance. Then she heard it again: softer, not quite as clear, but not far away, surely, if she could only pinpoint the exact location. Down past the fake lake, past Scott's elementary school, just behind the volunteer firehouse, right *there*, it must be. She ran indoors, changed her pajamas for jeans and an oversized *Northern Exposure* T-shirt, grabbed up her hiking boots—only putting them on when she was outside once more—and set off down the street, following the music.

It led her on, teasing her the way she used to tease her Aunt Isabela's cat with a crumpled ball of paper dangled on a string, just out of reach. The shivering slide of Indigo's horn—*it must be, what else could it be?*—led her on through the breathless California night; sometimes she thought she heard a second horn sporting and pouncing madly around the melody like Aunt Isabela's cat; now and then she would have sworn that there were a dozen of them, coming and going across harmonies and countermelodies that seized her heart and froze her breath. *The music I hear in my head, always, all my life, the music I can never name . . . .*

The streets were empty under an orange half-moon, except for a few cars that she could hear blocks away because of their thudding stereos echoing between the houses. Strangely, they failed to drown out the music, even when they were close enough for the drivers to study her, yell something insulting, and speed away. Joey paid no attention to them but hurried along, turning left or right whenever the music sounded nearer down a certain street. It never altogether ceased again, but it ebbed and flowed so inconstantly that she bent her utmost attention to homing in on its source. For that reason, she never noticed precisely where she was when she first crossed the Border.

It was dawn there, on the other side. Between one step and the next, it was dawn.

JOEY STOPPED WITH ONE FOOT still off the ground, just about to come down. Very slowly she lowered it, not onto asphalt but onto cool, springy morning bracken. She looked at her feet in the grass for a long time; then raised her head to stare up at a sky like none she had ever seen. It might have been the sky over another planet: not because of its color or the shape of its apricot ruffle of cloud, but because she was seeing it through air so clear that everything appeared slightly brighter and nearer than it really was. Joey felt dazedly that she could have squeezed the rising sun and plucked it for her breakfast.

The suburban streets she knew had vanished utterly. She was standing on a low rise of ground, surrounded by tall blue trees stretching away in three directions. The trees looked like oaks of some sort, as nearly as Joey could ever tell anything about trees, but their leaves were a deeper blue than the sky itself, the color of Indigo's suddenly remembered eyes. Beyond the trees she glimpsed green hills one way—higher ones, these—the least glint of sun on water another, and in a third a bright expanse of meadowland, soft with wildflowers. *Whatever wild means in this place. No houses, no roads, no people anywhere. Maybe everything's wild here.*

It was the music that kept her from being frightened. The

music was everywhere now, distinctly closer, yet still impossible to pin down to any one location. It surged and softened continually, even here, joyous and irresponsible, seeming to bubble out of stones, like the voice of a spring; to chirp up from grass and earth, like insect fiddling; to tumble down upon her like rain. Putting everything else off but the music, to be reacted to and dealt with later, she cast about quickly, making several false starts, and finally decided to move toward the open meadow, away from the trees. *I'll hear it better there, zero in on it. I'll find it. It wants me to find it.*

She was well into the meadow, following the music through sea-green, shin-high grass and pausing to investigate flowers that looked like long orange tongues and shiny ebony buttons, when the music stopped abruptly. The shock was almost a physical one: she wheeled, staring wildly around her. Heavy and cold as a snake, shadow touched the back of her neck.

The wide meadow itself seemed to draw back, crouching away from her in every direction, darkening wherever she looked, leaving her standing dreadfully exposed to something she could not comprehend. The shadow was moving too fast and passing too high overhead for her to be sure of anything except that it was made of a multitude of small flying creatures—*but they aren't birds, they aren't birds*—and that they chattered to one another as they flew, making a tiny, cold, clicking sound. Joey turned and ran for the trees.

The shadow turned too, almost on the instant; she could feel the dark swirl on her skin without looking back. *Oh God, I shouldn't have moved, they've seen me.* The soft grass dragged at her heavy hiking boots now, the orange-and-black flowers clawed her legs and ankles, and behind her the cold chattering drew closer while the blue trees appeared as faraway as ever. Her head was full of the terrible sound. She stumbled with every stride, tottering desperately to keep from falling; breathing had become like swallowing fire. She felt the shadow slanting down across her heart.

With one last lurching bound she lunged into a different shadow, sheltering and sweet-smelling, and fell flat on her face. She was up in an instant, reeling on a few more yards before she fell again. Even then she was clutching at tree roots, dragging herself forward, when she heard the voice at her ear. It said, "Be still, daughter. Be very still."

For one moment it seemed to Joey that the sound pursuing her had formed itself into words, words that would likely be the last she would ever hear. But the voice said, "The trees will stop them, I think," and she realized that there was no greedy click to this sound, no freezing eagerness. It was a lightly gruff voice saying, "They don't like the trees"; then, when she started to raise her head, "*Down!* Be *still!*"

Joey lay obediently motionless, though her eyes were full of dirt and a root was digging painfully into her side. The shadow was withdrawing slowly—she could feel it, even while she heard the angry chattering still crackling above her like heat lightning. When she moved a trapped arm slightly and the voice did not reprimand her, she was emboldened to turn her head in the direction it had come from. At first she saw nothing, though her nose began to become aware of a warmly pungent smell, absurdly familiar, *like the bathrooms at school after they've just been cleaned.* Then she saw him.

He was a head or more shorter than she, and he so perfectly suited the illustrations Joey had seen in books of mythology that she had to fight back laughter as sudden as a sneeze. He smiled crookedly at her, showing square berry-stained teeth between

bearded lips. His brown, triangular face was human, except for the pointed ears—really pointed, much more so than Indigo's —and the yellow goat eyes with their slit horizontal pupils. His legs were a goat's split-foot legs, just as the book had shown them, bending backward in a sharp hock where human knees would be. He was naked, his chest, belly, and legs alike covered with coarse dark hair, straight and matted with dirt; but the hair of his head curled so tightly that it all but hid the two small horns peeping through. His smile widened as Joey gaped at him.

"My name is Ko," he announced. "You need not feel shy about admiring me." He smoothed his beard with grubby, broken-nailed fingers and added, "I was prettier when I was young, but lacked the quality of mature experience that I have now."

Joey found words at last, though they came out only in a painful croak. "I *know* what you are, I saw a picture. You're a faun or something—a satyr, that's it. You're a real satyr."

Ko looked mildly puzzled. "Is that what I would be called in your world?" He tried the word over once or twice, then shrugged. "Well enough for Outworlders, I suppose. All in what you're accustomed to, no doubt."

"Those things," Joey whispered. Ko understood her immediately. "*Perytons,* we call them here, as my folk call ourselves the *tirujai.* You did very well indeed to escape them, daughter. Not many do. I would stay where you are for a bit, and speak softly. They are very patient creatures, *perytons.*"

Joey obeyed him, though she wriggled by degrees into a more comfortable position, getting her elbows under her. She asked the satyr, "You said *in your world.* If I'm . . . if I'm really not in my own world . . . okay, where am I?" She held her breath, not at all sure that she wanted to hear the answer.

Ko said, "You are in Shei'rah." To Joey, that first time, the word felt like a small breeze against her cheek. She actually put up a hand to touch her face, saying, "I'm *where?*"

"This is Shei'rah," the satyr repeated. "I should tell you straightaway that you are not the first Outworlder to find the way here. But you are the first in a very long while, and I am most pleased to meet you. I always like them, Outworlders."

The chattering of the *perytons* was receding slowly—Joey had to strain to hear it now. She sat up and made an attempt to brush the dirt out of her hair and eyes. She said carefully, "My name is Josephine Angelina Rivera. People call me Joey. I live on Alomar Street, in a town called Woodmont, only it's not a real town, more like a big jumbly mall west of L.A. My mother's in real estate, and my father does something with computers, electronics. I have a brother who's a total dork, and a grandmother who's in one of those places for old people, which I wish she wasn't. I go to Ridgecrest Junior High School. I have to see the dentist day after tomorrow. What am I doing in a place with a name like Shei'rah?" She looked from the satyr's inquisitive face to the blue trees all around, to the ground where a crimson snail the size of a softball peered back at her. "I mean, I'm supposed to be in bed," she said softly.

The music had begun once more, though Joey could not have said just when. Satyrs played funny little pipes, she remembered, *bamboo or something,* but Ko's hands seemed mostly to be occupied in scratching himself; and besides, the music was coming from very far off this time. Ko stretched—he did smell seriously funky, no question—scratched his bottom luxuriously until his jaunty tuft of a tail went round and round like a propellor, and finally said, "Well, I should think we would be safe enough now. Shall we go, daughter?"

The absurdity of the word, coming again from such a creature, made Joey giggle in spite of herself. She said, "Go? Go where?"

Ko raised his bushy, slanted eyebrows. "Why, to see the Eldest, where else? The Eldest will know what to do."

"The Eldest?" Joey got to her feet. "What Eldest?" Ko smiled without answering. Joey said, "I can't *go* anywhere—I've got school tomorrow, I've got a *test*, for God's sake. And my parents, if they wake up and I'm just gone like this. . . . Look, I don't know how I got here, but there has to be a way back. Just point me back the way I came, and I'll be fine. I really have to go home, I'm sorry."

The satyr's smile became gently pitying. "Daughter, you cannot cross the Border now. The moon is already gone."

"Border," Joey said. "What border? What's the moon got to do with anything? What are you talking about?"

But Ko was already moving off through the trees. Joey scrambled after him, desperate not to be left behind. "I have to get *home*!" she shouted when she caught up with him. "I have to be in *school*! How far is it to this Eldest, whoever *that* is?"

Ko turned and took her hand, patting it with fingers that felt as thick and scratchy as a dog's pad. "We will chat as we go," he said. "All will be well, daughter, I am very nearly sure of it. All is quite often well in Shei'rah."

Chapter Three

The journey took them all day. Ko avoided the meadowland altogether—"This close to the Border, an open field is a dinner invitation for the *perytons.*"— and kept to cover at all times, no matter how rough the track became. He led Joey through wood after brambly thicket after dim, deep wood again, the undergrowth broken only occasionally by sun-flecked clearings where birds, as impossibly bright as though her little brother had colored them, sang like wind over water and water over stone. A pair of small black-and-gold birds followed them for a time, diving and wheeling around Ko's head, trilling constantly into his hairy ears. He never actually answered them, which vaguely relieved Joey, but he was definitely listening.

At moments Joey was certain beyond question that they were being watched closely as they traveled. At first she would halt suddenly and snap her head around, but there was never anything to see, and the act brought back thoughts of Abuelita teasing her to try looking in her own ear one more time. Thinking

37

of Abuelita made her sad, so she stopped turning around; but she continued to feel herself being surveyed, studied, intensely considered, perhaps by the blue trees, perhaps by the wind.

A bright brook ran through one of the glades and Joey dropped to her knees beside it, calling to Ko to wait for her. The water was cold and sweet; the taste of it spread shiveringly through her. Leaning forward to drink again, she saw her face, dark and bony and *ordinary*, and stuck out her tongue at it, as she always did. But this time, this time, another face floated up behind, under, through her own, shattering her image into a giggle of bubbles, sticking out its pointed green tongue at her and laughing with utterly shameless joy, like the unceasing music itself. Joey shrieked, leaped to her feet, and dashed frantically after the satyr, whom she almost knocked down as she careened into him. He steadied her with rough, startlingly powerful hands, saying, "Calm yourself, daughter, old Ko is here. What has frightened you so?"

Joey told him, and was outraged when he promptly burst out laughing himself, bending double to clap his hands and slap his goat thighs. "Child," he gasped when he could speak again, "daughter, that was a brook-*jalla* you saw, nothing more. Harmless as ditch-minnows, they are, and just as common, never pay them any heed. Vulgar notions of humor." Turning suddenly sober, he added, "The ones in the rivers, those are another matter. A full-grown river-*jalla* would have drowned you deep and picked your bones by now. Never go near a riverbank, not ever, unless you are with me, or with the Eldest. Do you understand me, daughter?"

"Yes," Joey whispered; and then, "Why do you always call me that, *daughter*? I mean, about the one thing I know for sure right now is I'm not your daughter." Fearing that the satyr would take offense, she added hurriedly, "I mean, it's cool, no problem, it's just I'm just *not*."

Ko smiled, his yellow eyes turning momentarily to a warm gold, sparkling with tiny darknesses. "When you are one hundred and eighty-seven years old, as I am," he replied, "you are entitled to call anyone you choose anything you like. I call you daughter because it pleases me to do so, and for no other reason. Come, it is a long way yet to the Eldest. Walk with me."

Joey stayed close to his side as they traveled on: back into the shelter of the blue trees for a while, and then out into comparatively open country, marked by groves of much smaller, more delicate-looking trees, set like colored-glass ornaments among low hills splashed with blossoms. Joey recognized none of the flowers, but their smell was so distantly, achingly familiar that it made her think of Abuelita again. Abuelita, who talked too loudly, because she was growing deaf, and deliberately spoke more and more Spanish as Joey's parents spoke less and less. Abuelita, who loved all music, especially her granddaughter's, and who smelled better than anyone in the world.

Joey stood still, thinking, *A whole country that smells like Abuelita. Oh now, now I'm homesick, I wasn't paying attention before. Abuelita, you got me into this, some way, I don't know how. You be all right till I get back. You hear me, Abuelita?*

Running to catch up with Ko, she was brought up short by his outflung arm. He was pointing silently to an outcrop of rocks directly ahead of them. A white snake was unhurriedly crossing the path. It was thicker than Joey's leg, though no longer, and it was the color of city snow, and it had two heads. The one at the tail appeared to be asleep; in any event, its eyes were closed and it dragged along through the dust with the rest of the body. But the gleaming black eyes of the head in front were wide awake, glaring sideways at Joey and the satyr with a warning contempt as the white serpent advanced. Ko took a single deliberate step toward it: instantly a red heat spread out from the centers of the creature's eyes, and the head reared swiftly on its burly neck to show long fangs oozing a transparent gray slime. Ko backed away, and the snake moved on into the underbrush at the side of the path. Joey could hear the slow crackling of its passage even after it was gone from sight.

"A *jakhao*," Ko said. "Nobody really likes them."

He started ahead briskly, but Joey stayed where she was, because her legs had stopped working. "That thing had two heads," she shouted after him. "Two heads!"

"It was a *jakhao*, I told you," the satyr answered over his shoulder. "Hurry along, daughter."

"I'm not your daughter!" Joey screamed. "I don't belong here! I'm supposed to be asleep in bed in my room, *my* room. I don't belong anywhere they've got satyrs and two-headed snakes and flying things that chase you and try to kill you, and I don't even know what they are!" She realized that she was hysterical, but the knowledge felt as faraway as home. "What kind of a *place* is this, and who's playing that *music*? I was just trying to find the music, that's all I was trying to do." She felt tears on her face and was furious about it, but they kept on falling.

Ko turned and once again studied her expressionlessly for a moment. Then he came back toward her, and silently put his arms around her. His horned head came awkwardly against her chest, the rough hair of his arms rasped her skin, and at close quarters he stank worse than Kenny Rowles who sat next to her in math class. But he held her quite gently, and Joey put her own arms around his back and cried until she stopped.

When she did stop, Ko put her a little away and said, "This is

Shei'rah, I told you that. It is a world like your world, like the many and many that slip by each other among the stars." He patted her shoulder. "More than that, I do not know. But I am taking you where you may learn."

Joey sniffled. "My parents'll wake up and think I'm dead. They'll think I got kidnapped, the way it happens all the time." She almost started to cry again, but held it back. "All right," she said. "All right. We're off to see the Eldest, let's do it. All right."

The road rose and fell with the hills as they walked, but even so it was easier going than the woodland had been. The sky was so intensely blue that Joey could hardly bear to look up: she thought she might begin falling upward if she did that, tumbling into the sky forever. She asked Ko about the *perytons*. "I just saw a kind of cloud that came at me, making that awful noise they make. I couldn't tell you what one of them actually looks like."

"We never say *one peryton*," the satyr replied thoughtfully. "We have no—no imagining for it, a *peryton* by itself. They travel always in vast swarms, packs—clouds, as you say—and they hunt anything that moves, and what they catch they devour on the spot. They leave nothing, nothing—there is a saying that the *perytons* even eat your shadow." Joey remembered the freezing weight of the *perytons'* own shadow on her shoulders, and shivered a little.

"Okay, never mind the *perytons*," she said. "The what's-it in the water, the *jalla* thing, and the snake with the two heads, whatever you called it. And the—" She gaped at a sudden stroke of gold-and-scarlet lightning across the dizzyingly clear sky, and then realized that it was a bird, a bird flying so fast that it was out of sight by the time Joey understood that what had felt like a white-hot brand across her eyes was only beauty. "And that, that!" she wailed, "*that*! What kind of a place is this? Everything you look at, it either scares you to death or it breaks your heart. I mean, what kind of a *place*?"

"That was a *miri*," Ko said, unperturbed. "How lucky you were to see it on your first day in Shei'rah. There is never more than one *miri* at a time, and when they grow old they set their nests afire and burn themselves to ashes. And when the fire dies down, there is a new young *miri*. What do you think of that, daughter?"

Joey was trembling. "A phoenix," she whispered. "That's a phoenix. We read about them in school. But they're imaginary, they're legends. Like satyrs, or whatever you call yourself."

Ko shrugged and scratched. "The Eldest will explain it to you."

"Oh, right," Joey said heavily. "The Eldest. You better tell me about the Eldest, we're dragging our butts all this way to see him."

"To see *them*, daughter!" Ko laughed with pure pleasure, and took her hand. "I cannot tell you what the Eldest are," he continued. "They are themselves, they have always been themselves, all three kinds. I have no other word for them. They are the Eldest."

"You're a hundred and eighty-something years old," Joey said. "And *they're* the Eldest?" Ko nodded happily. "And there are three different kinds of them?" She had visions of TV aliens with huge, varyingly wrinkled bald skulls.

"One kind is like the sky," Ko answered. "There is another kind that is like fire, and one that is earth, like earth. But they are all the Eldest."

Joey sighed. "Great," she said. "Tell me one thing, anyway. Are the Eldest—are they the ones making the music? That music out there."

As she spoke, a single horn, suddenly sounding as near as Ko himself, tossed up a melody as graceful and sad as the long fall of a leaf; caught it once, bore it aloft just a little way more, then let it go where it would go. Ko said in the silence, "Daughter, no, the Eldest do not make music. The Eldest *are* the music." Joey did not answer.

The road was climbing steadily now, slanting across a narrow valley dotted with thorn trees whose triangular leaves flashed silver in the sunlight. The music rose and fell as it chose, weaving itself like a flowering vine through the soft scrape of Ko's cloven hooves on the road. Sometimes there seemed to be only one or two horns playing; sometimes at least four; sometimes there might have been a dozen, more, an orchestra of Indigos. Joey tried to hear it with John Papas's trained, knowing ears, and could not.

A group of small creatures dozing atop a sunny boulder roused to watch them go by. Joey noticed almost casually that they looked rather like pictures of dragons, except for being no more than six inches long and sand-colored as the rocks where they crouched. When Joey's eyes met the hooded eyes of the largest, it hissed minute defiance and spread tawny little wings protectively above the other dragonlets. Ko said, "*Shendi*, early this year," as though he were commenting in pleased surprise on spring flowers.

Ko picked fruit for her along the way—sweet, heavy purple figs, and something that he called a *javadur*. It looked like a cross between a mango and an avocado, smelled like a wet dog, and tasted like butterscotch custard. Joey—who had had nothing since her midnight glass of chocolate milk in another world—devoured as many *javadurs* as Ko could find, and asked for more. The satyr was delighted, telling her, "Stop here and rest, daughter. The best *javadurs* grow deeper in the wood. These are but their shadows, you will see. Wait for me."

Joey flopped down gratefully with her back against a tree with pleasantly bumpy bark like a great golden pineapple. She fell asleep instantly, and dreamed of BeeBee Huang, her best friend at school. The two of them were bathing her little brother Scott, for some dreamy reason, and BeeBee was saying that they had to be very careful because weird things sometimes hid right in the soap bubbles, and they could get up Scott's nose so he couldn't breathe. Joey had heard worse possibilities in her life. She was starting to say so when she became aware that she was having more and more trouble breathing herself. There was a smell like burning garbage in her own nose, and her neck hurt a lot in a faraway sort of way. Scott and BeeBee had vanished, but someone was shouting loudly somewhere in a voice she almost knew. Joey opened her eyes.

A cold, scratchy hand was covering her mouth tightly; other hands were clamped painfully under her arms. Not until the tree branch bumped her head did she realize that she was off the ground, being hauled steadily upward with implacable strength. The angry voice was still shouting, and the golden leaves all around her were hissing and rattling—*or were those other voices?* She had a moment to register that the hand on her mouth was rough with scales before it and all the rest let go, and she tumbled through the stubby branches to sprawl on bare ground. Just for a moment she saw faces looking down after her, golden themselves, with hard green eyes: reptilian faces, but flattened instead of pointed, their ears absurdly like those of teddy bears. Then the boughs closed over them, and they were gone.

When Joey finally caught her breath, which seemed to take forever, she sat up, drawing breath to scream for Ko. Then she stopped, still gaping, because she was staring straight into Indigo's hot blue eyes. He was crouched beside her, unworldly-beautiful as ever, but somehow made almost human by the anger with which he addressed her. "What is the matter with you, Outworld child? Do you have no sense at all, then?"

Joey shook her head dazedly, rubbing the back of her neck and shoulders. She hurt everywhere, and she was beginning to shiver violently. Indigo said, "No more sense than to sleep under a *cryak* tree. You are luckier than you deserve that I was by."

"What are you doing here?" Joey whispered. "Where's Ko? I want Ko."

The boy snorted, sounding astonishingly like John Papas. He started to speak, but the satyr was already there, his ropy arms tight and smelly and comforting around her. "Here I am, daughter, here's old Ko, and here you are with no harm done, only rest a little." But his voice was trembling almost as badly as she was.

"Rest a little," Indigo mimicked him brutally. "Rest under a *cryak*, like dinner served up on a fresh green leaf. What possessed you, *tiruja*, to let her sleep there?"

Ko bowed his head, his voice barely audible. "I thought . . . the talk was that they were gone from here. They wander so, the *criyaqui*, you know that—they have not been seen in this wood for three seasons, four . . ." The last words trailed away miserably in Joey's hair.

"They have returned," Indigo said. "As the *tirujai* should know before anyone." Joey looked back and forth between him and Ko. The satyr's voice was stronger when he spoke to her again. "Daughter, I do not ask you to forgive me. Only . . . only I did truly think these trees were safe. I did think so."

"What are they?" Joey asked shakily. "Why did they—I

mean, what did they *want?*" She could still see the flat, avid snake eyes in the golden faces, even when she closed her own eyes.

"No one knows," Ko answered her. "No one taken by the *criyaqui* ever returns. They live in those trees, and they take my folk when they can, from the branches, as they almost had you. We never find bones or—or anything, so we never know. . . ." He held Joey so tightly that new places started hurting.

"I don't believe this," Joey said. "That's it, that's all, that simple. I just don't believe any of this is happening. You either," she said to Ko, but she buried her face in his stinky hair anyway.

She heard Indigo ask the satyr, "Where are you taking her?" and heard Ko's reply, "To the Eldest, of course. Where would I bring an Outworlder?"

Indigo sounded oddly subdued when he spoke again. "They are not—" He paused, and then said, even more quietly, "You know how they are beset, the Eldest?"

"They are still who they are," Ko answered with startling fierceness over Joey's head. "You know better than I that all things change in Shei'rah but the Eldest. I see them no differently, trust their understanding no less than I ever did."

Indigo did not speak again for some time. There was an uncharacteristic weariness in his voice when he said finally, "I should certainly know better than to talk with a *tiruja* about the Eldest. Take her where you will, then, but at least you might keep her away from *cryak* trees. There is an old man on the other side of the Border who would be grateful." Joey did not hear him leave.

"I am so sorry, daughter," Ko said wretchedly, as Joey began to turn her head back and forth to see if her neck still worked. "If it had not been for Indigo . . ."

"How'd he get here, anyway?" Joey demanded. "Did he follow me across the Border or something?"

Ko smiled then, despite his obvious misery. "Did I not tell you the Border has its wanderers in both directions? There are some few of Shei'rah who know your world almost as well as you do, perhaps."

"Indigo's from here," Joey said slowly. "From Shei'rah." She shook her head again, thumping one ear lightly with the heel of her hand, as though there were water in it. "Should have figured *that* one out by now, shouldn't I? Anybody who looks like that. Right." She stood up, scrubbing at her mouth to rid it of the sour chill of the *criyaqui* hands. "Okay. Onward."

TOWARD EVENING the long road finally began to level off, and Joey made out the smudge of a wood on the horizon. Distant as it was, she could see that these trees were not blue, nor golden either, but red: no autumn scarlet but a deep ruby color, trunk and leaves, almost black in the late light. *As though they had blood in them, like people, not that chlorophyll stuff.* As they drew nearer, she realized that the forest was much larger than any they had passed through that day, and that Ko was guiding her straight into its darkly glowing heart. "The Eldest live here," he said. "We may find them or we may not, but this is their home."

"We may *not*?" Joey echoed him. "Oh, that's wonderful. My folks have the FBI and the TAC Squad out looking for me by now, Mr. Papas won't know what's happened to me, I'm missing a major, major math exam—it's a quarter of your grade right there—and my brother Scott's probably already moved all his stuff into my room. And you're telling me we might not even *find* the people who can get me home?"

"I said the Eldest will know what to do," the satyr replied. "Believe me, daughter, whether we see them or not makes no difference at all. They will still know what is best for Shei'rah."

"For Shei'rah?" Joey demanded. "How about what's best for *me*?"

"It will be the same," Ko said, speaking more confidently than he had since Joey's encounter with the *criyaqui*. But he was silent after that, and his voice was thinner and less assured when he spoke again. "The Eldest . . . it is a little as Indigo said. You must remember—they are perhaps not quite what they were. Only perhaps, mind you."

Joey let her arms flap against her sides in exasperation. "I don't even know what they *are*!" But the music danced up from the depths of the red forest, strong and strange, making a kind of sense inside her that nothing she could remember ever had. She said, "Okay. Okay, whatever, Ko." It was the first time she had called the satyr by his name.

The red forest—Ko said it was called Sundown Wood—felt like a living thing to Joey from the moment she and Ko passed under the outermost trees. The lowest boughs towered high above her, their shadows warm against her face, and wherever she put her foot down, the forest floor seemed to throb in response. The music of Shei'rah seemed to be pulsing, not only everywhere she turned to look or listen, but in herself as well, speaking deeply to her in the secret place where she made up music of her own. She felt herself cupped kindly between vast ruby hands, and breathed on.

SUNDOWN WOOD NEVER fully darkened, no matter how far Joey and Ko pressed into it. The sun had actually set by now, but the forest continued to glow from within, never growing chill. In the luminous calm she heard the anxious scuttle of very small feet, the silent sigh of wide wings overhead, and a heavy, deliberate *pad-pad-pad* close by that would have terrified her anywhere else. But the satyr tugged at her hand, telling her, "This way now, daughter," and the music murmured, "This way, this way." Joey followed.

And then the red trees fell away, parting like tall grass before the wind, and Joey and Ko emerged into a clearing under a sky swirling with stars as thickly as though it were snowing in Sundown Wood. The Eldest stood waiting in the center of the glade.

One was as grand and old as the trees themselves, and so black that night paled around him. Another, blue-gray as a storm cloud, calmed the eye with her presence; the third was more slender, longer-bodied, with a graceful tuft of beard, looking as though she were made of seafoam embroidered with green phosphorescence. They stood together with their heads high, their beautiful tails floating like ghosts on the red night air, and their long seashell horns blossoming in the starlight. The music flowered about them.

Joey's heart thumped once and turned over to see their eyes. They were swollen shut, the eyes of all three Eldest, covered so thickly with a blue-green encrustation that they looked almost bejeweled. Joey realized that the Eldest were blind.

Chapter Four

*J*oey awoke in sunlight, curled on her side under a red tree, with soft boughs pulled over her for warmth, and two unicorns looking down at her. One was the unicorn with the look of being somehow not quite as solid as the others, but more a creation of sea and wind. The other was much smaller, the color of starlight; dancy and fidgety, too young for mobility, too restless to be regal. It was the light drumming of its forefeet in place that had wakened her. Joey caught her breath to realize that its moon-colored eyes showed the first light dusting of the encrustation that had blinded the three great Eldest.

The smaller unicorn said eagerly, "Mother, there, see? She's awake!"

Joey sat up, shaking leaves out of her hair. "Hello," she said, her voice hoarse and cracking, the way it always was in the morning. "Where's Ko?"

The second unicorn came forward, moving in a deliberate quicksilver flow. Blindness did not seem to burden her step, nor keep her from looking directly at Joey. She said, "I am Fireez, and this is Touriq, my son. Have you slept well?" Her voice was low and light, with a glint of humor just below the surface.

"I think so," Joey said. "Had a lot of crazy dreams, only I'm not sure they were dreams." She paused, then said slowly, "You're the Eldest. Ko told me."

"We are eldest of the Eldest," Fireez answered. "Except *him*." She nodded at her son, who was investigating Joey's hiking boots. Where his horn brushed against them the mud and dirt crumbled away, and they took on the luster of the horn itself. Joey said, "There was a black one."

Fireez's voice dropped slightly. "That was the Lord Sinti."

Touriq broke in excitedly, "You fell asleep, and he carried you here on his back! Sinti *never* does that! He lives all alone, no one ever *sees* Sinti, hardly ever—*I* never saw him before, until last night. You must be *very* important, for an Outworlder—"

"Touriq," his mother said, and no more, but the young unicorn was instantly still. Fireez said, "The Lord Sinti is eldest of all. We have no word for what he is." She laughed then—a sudden, absurd, wondrous little gurgle—and added, "Forgive my rudeness, but I also cannot help wondering what passed between you when he brought you here. Did he speak to you at all?"

Joey got stiffly to her feet. "I don't remember. Maybe." She began to smile, then stoppped sharply, saying, "No, that was in the dream, I know that for sure. I thought he was asking something about Abuelita, my grandmother. Had to be the dream, no way—I mean, how could he know about her, here in Shei'rah?"

"The Lord Sinti knows *everything*!" Touriq burst out, and his mother echoed him more sedately. "I think for age and wisdom like that of the Lord Sinti, such things as Borders have little meaning anymore." She nudged Touriq, who was fidgeting his forefeet again, and was clearly about to interrupt her. "Now my son is foolish and unmannerly, being less than two centuries old—"

"Wait," Joey said. "Wait, wait, I'm sorry, excuse me. *Centuries?*" She stared at the two of them: the son limitlessly eager, impudent as a sparrow; the mother all slow-surging grace, sea white, yet shivering constantly between sea blue and sea green, the excrescences clinging to her eyes seeming a wicked mockery of her natural color.

"We do not die," Fireez answered her quietly. "We can be killed, but we do not die naturally, as even the *tirujai* do. We have never even grown ill—not until now."

"Your eyes, you mean," Joey said. "You really can't see? All of you?" She pointed at Touriq, who was now strutting around proudly with one of her boots dangling by its laces from the tip of his horn. "I mean, *he* can see just fine."

"I see better than anybody," Touriq bragged. Fireez hushed him again, saying, "Most of our youngest still have their vision, but not all. It has come on us only recently—not long before Touriq was born—and even the Lord Sinti has not yet fathomed the cause. He will tell you more of this than I can."

Joey took a deep breath. She said, "Centuries," shook herself once, and began struggling into her boots, while the unicorns waited, gravely curious about everything she might do. Finally she faced them, sighed, and said, "I don't guess there's a chance that I had an accident when I left my house last night, and I'm really in the hospital in like intensive care?" Touriq looked in puzzlement at his mother. Joey sighed again. "I didn't think so. Okay, it's all really real, and I'm here, and you guys really are unicorns, and you live forever. Only, if you can't see me, how do you know I'm here?"

Touriq looked in puzzlement at his mother. Fireez answered gently, "We feel your presence. You cast a shadow in our minds, as a tree does, or a bird, or water. We have learned to move so, between shadow and shadow. In the same way, we do not make words with our mouths, as you do, and as Ko and the other *tirujai* do. We speak with our minds. You are hearing us in your mind."

Ko appeared then, his hairy arms laden as high as his chin with bright, fragrant fruit. Joey recognized only the *javadurs*, of the rest, she chose a couple of round red things that looked a bit like blood oranges (though they tasted like bananas) and another that was dusty-purple as a plum, with a flavor of fermented melons. Ko greeted the two unicorns with formal politeness and informed Joey, "When you are done with your breakfast, the Lord Sinti waits for you."

"Oh. Oh, okay. I guess." Joey gulped the fruit quickly, wiped her mouth and waited for Ko to take the lead. But the satyr shook his head, saying, "Walk where you choose, and he will be there."

Touriq nipped at his mother's cloudy mane. "Can I go with her? I want to see Sinti too, can I go?"

"When he wants you, you will know," Fireez replied. Joey looked back and forth between the unicorns and the satyr. She said quietly at last, "Centuries. Oh, boy." She turned then, chose a path, and walked away into the trees.

SUNDOWN WOOD WAS MURMURING contentedly to itself in the early sun. The air smelled to Joey like fresh-washed laundry drying on the line; the trees and the pale-brown earth faintly of cinnamon. When she halted to lean close against a huge red bole she felt its life surging through the furry bark under her shoulder. Just above her, a small bird as golden as gift wrapping sang with such simple passion that even the magic music Joey had followed into Shei'rah fell silent. A lavender-green creature like a cross between a newt and a praying mantis perched on her right foot, looking up at her, its eyes too steadily aware for what it was. "Hello," Joey said. "You talk in my head too?" But the creature darted away as soon as she spoke. Joey walked on.

She never saw the black unicorn until he was pacing by her side. The other three had been the size of deer, but he was tall enough that she had to tilt her head back to meet his eyes, cruelly jeweled as those of the Lady Fireez. Blind or not, they drew her own gaze so deep and far that she forgot her feet, stumbled, and had to steady herself against his flank. Beneath the almost shocking warmth of him—*unicorns look cool but they sure put out body heat*—Joey could feel laughter she could not hear, like a cat's silent purr. He smelled like oranges.

"I have to go home," she said. "That's the main thing. I mean, I like it here, it's really beautiful and everything, and I wouldn't mind staying awhile, but I ought to start home."

Sinti's voice flowed slowly through her from head to foot, like the water of Shei'rah. "I can show you the way."

Joey stopped walking. "You can? But Ko said I couldn't get home because the Border had shifted or something. I don't get it. How can a border move?"

The black unicorn looked down at her, his horn a slash of midnight under the red morning trees. "Because Shei'rah moves."

He was silent for a while before he spoke again, dropping his words carefully into Joey's own dazed silence. "There are many and many worlds, but our Shei'rah is bound to your world in some way that I do not understand even now. We float beside it, we slip over it, like the shadow of a cloud. We may stay in one place for a day, or for a thousand years—it is Shei'rah that chooses. But there is always a Border, and who truly feels our music may cross it, from either side, on any night when the moon is high. Nothing more is needed to pass in and out of Shei'rah—only deep desire, and the music, and a bit of the moon."

"That's wild," Joey whispered. "Oh, that is so *wild*." She stopped abruptly, digging both hands into her hair. "Oh, my God, how long have I been here? I can't keep track of time, I don't know why, my parents'll be *crazy*, I got to go *now*."

Again Sinti's gentle amusement resounded in her own body, though she was not touching him. "Time is different in Shei'rah. When you do return, you will not have been missed. I promise you this."

"Wait," Joey said. "Wait, wait, wait, *wait*. You're saying I can stay here for however long, and when I get home it'll still be last night? Wow, I'm sorry, I don't mean to be disrespectful, but that's weird. My stomach gets funny just thinking about it."

Sinti did not answer her. Joey walked along beside him, trying to concentrate only on the music. Clearer and closer by far in the presence of unicorns, it yet remained curiously elusive, lilting up impudently from creeks and stones and red trees, dancing where it chose. She asked hesitantly, "Why are you guys all going blind? I mean *centuries*, you'd think somebody could work it out."

"It is to do with your world," the black unicorn said. "With the connection, the bond between us. That is all I know, all I can see, and it is not enough." The voice inside her was quietly resonant with bitterness. "I am Sinti, I am Eldest of the Eldest, I am supposed to be wise beyond wisdom. I have never failed my folk, never once failed Shei'rah. More of them lose their sight every day, yet they live still in perfect confidence that I will discover a remedy. And I cannot help them, nor help myself. I cannot help them."

"I'm sorry," Joey said. "I really am. They do all kinds of things with eyes now in—in my world, but I guess that wouldn't help you a lot. In Shei'rah."

Sinti said nothing more, and they went on together. Joey saw Sundown Wood warming and ripening before the black unicorn: she saw unknown flowers hurrying to open, spied the beasts and half-beasts who crouched in the underbrush to watch the Lord Sinti pass; and she heard the forest itself making a sound almost too low to hear.

Sinti halted abruptly, and again Joey felt the sweet, unnerving giddiness that comes with looking long into the eyes of the Eldest, whether they can see you or not. He said, "Listen to me. There is a thing about us that some mortal should know. Listen well, Josephine Angelina Rivera."

In his silent voice, her name rippled and chimed as Joey had never imagined it could do. She nodded meekly, and Sinti said, "We can change our shape. We can look like you."

Joey nodded meekly. Sinti went on, "Not often, never often. I have not Changed for a very long time, and most of our folk forget they can do it at all. But it is so—we can take the human form and cross the Border into your world, and sometimes we do. You have met the Eldest before, Josephine Rivera."

Through the trees, behind his high shoulder, Joey glimpsed movement and a wide greenness, and heard the music of Shei'rah sporting beyond. Sinti went on, "Through all your history, there have always been some few of us moving among you. Most remain only a little while, a moment of your time, just long enough to be glimpsed and disbelieved and never forgotten. But there are others, a few . . . have you not encountered legends of immortal wanderers, known in different places under different names, human lifetimes apart? Eldest, those were, scholars and explorers and mapmakers of your world. Yet these too come home to Shei'rah in time, as they must. Your world kills us, most sooner, some later. We can never forget that."

Joey thought of the boy Indigo, bright as a knife in the dimness of John Papas's music shop, playing the first shockingly joyous notes of the music that had drawn her out of one world and into another. She tried to find the courage to ask Sinti about Indigo, but the words would not come, and instead she blurted out, "When you—when the Eldest take our shape, what happens about the horns?"

"Our horns separate from us when we Change," Sinti answered. "We take them with us, always. We must, or we could never return home. And one of the Eldest who cannot return to Shei'rah will die."

Joey realized that she was suddenly cold, shivering hard in the tender morning sun of Shei'rah. "But if somebody lost his horn, or maybe sold it—"

The black unicorn had begun to walk on; now he turned and gazed down at her, and Joey was suddenly more frightened than she had been when the *perytons* pursued her. She took a step backwards, hearing him in herself again. "I do not know what *sold* is, Josephine Rivera."

He was gone then, as soundlessly as he had appeared, and so swiftly that Joey could not tell which way he had gone. She started to call after him, but the act felt strange and presumptuous. She hesitated only briefly before she turned and walked on alone, walking fast, looking straight ahead, until she came to the edge of Sundown Wood.

AND THERE, ON A SUNLIT PLAIN, bare of trees but alight with wildflowers, sprawling away and away toward sea-green hills and sea-blue hills beyond, Joey saw the Eldest. There were dozens of them, scores of them, and they were of every color, not merely white as Joey had only seen unicorns pictured, but brown, storm-gray, black like the Lord Sinti, deep red as the trees of Sundown Wood, even a few who were the golden-pink of dawn. Some grazing, some racing one another from nowhere to delighted nowhere, the youngest fencing with their small horns, aggressively playful; some gathered in small groups, heads resting on one another's backs, others standing perfectly apart and motionless—so they shone on the plain, filling and overflowing Joey's vision, as the music of their presence filled her heart. Dazzled, enchanted, mindless, she walked toward them.

The unicorns took no notice of her until she had drawn quite near. Heads came up one by one, and a widening ripple of sound spread out among them. It was no horse's shrill alarm-whinny, but a soft two-note call, quick and birdlike. A few curvetted sharply away from her, but most stood their ground or eased aside to let her pass. Two of the unicorns, however, made straight for her. They were of a kind she had not seen before: both red, as tall as Sinti, but notably bulkier, necks thick with muscle to support horns which must have been three feet long. Their hooves were bigger, their manes and tails heavier and coarser, and they made a low, warning sound as they came toward her.

"I'm Joey," she said aloud. "I'm a friend of Sinti—I mean, I know him." She stood very still.

The red unicorns stopped barely more than a horn's length from her. Up close, unlike the unicorns she had met so far, they had a strong, wild smell about them, raw as the lion cages at the zoo. They did not speak, but glanced at each other and back at Joey, the fierce sound deepening in their throats. Joey said, "I'm not hurting anything."

She never found out what the great creatures might have done, because a smaller figure pushed abruptly between them, and Fireez's son Touriq announced proudly in her mind, "There, I found you! Come on!"

As irresistible a force as her brother Scott, he nudged and prodded her like a tugboat, guiding her away from the two red unicorns. They made no move to interfere; but whenever she turned to look back at them, their suspicious eyes were still following her. Touriq said, "Don't mind them, they don't mean anything. *Karkadanns* are just like that."

"Wow, they're scary," Joey said. "I'm really glad you showed up. What did you call them?"

"*Karkadanns*," Touriq answered casually. He arched his neck and bumped his shoulder against Joey. He said, "Now we get to play. Climb up on my back."

"Climb *where?*" Touriq's shoulder stood no higher than Joey's own. "I'm too big," she said. "My legs are too long, I'll be too heavy. . . ."

"Climb up," Touriq repeated impatiently. "Tuck your legs along my sides and hold on, and don't worry. Come *on*, I want to show you to my friends!"

Joey gulped slightly, took a deep breath, and scrambled awkwardly onto Touriq's back, which felt wider than she had thought it would, and much stronger. She flattened herself against his neck and felt the astonishing swell of power as the unicorn colt gathered his slender legs under him and shot forward. He was at full gallop with his second stride, and Joey was horribly certain that he would collide with one or another of the unicorns grazing so tranquilly in his path. But most moved gracefully aside without looking up, while a handful of younger ones reared, wheeled, shrilled acceptance of his challenge, and raced after him. The bright field rang and shimmered under their hooves.

Joey sat up slowly, by very careful degrees. Touriq was moving so fast that her eyes burned from the tears whipped across them by the wind. The field was a blazing, streaming blur; the cloudburst rattle of the unicorns' hoofbeats drowned all other music. Through her tightly clamped legs she felt the deep ease of Touriq's stride, the calmness of his breathing, and understood that he was not even extending himself unusually. *He's playing. He's just playing.*

A silvery-gray unicorn moved up on Touriq's left, a black one on his right, but neither could pass him. Daring at last to turn her head, Joey looked back and gasped in wonder to see them all: Touriq's playmates and companions, a storm of colors, flooding over the plains of Shei'rah like spring. They called to one another as they ran, and Joey realized that she knew the high, haunting, skirling cries—that they were part of the music Indigo had played in Mr. Papas's shop, the music that had drawn her out of her bed to this place, this moment. She threw back her head, drummed her heels on Touriq's sides, and shrieked her own mad challenge into the wind.

The unicorns let the race carry them well into the surrounding foothills before they even began to slow down. Their pure pleasure, their joy in themselves, resounded through Joey: She felt herself thronged with voices, shining laughter, visions for which she had no words, and most of all music—the wild, prankish, frightening, endlessly reassuring music of Shei'rah. *Ko was right, it's their music. It's them.*

She slid off Touriq's back when he finally halted, and leaned against him, gasping and giggling. "That was wonderful," she managed to get out. "That was wonderful."

"I can run much faster than that," Touriq boasted innocently. "I outran a whole flock of *perytons* one time, when I was just little."

Joey looked anxiously up at the sky. Touriq, following her glance, said, "They never bother us when we're all together like this. Just if you're young and alone. Anyway, I'm not afraid of them."

"Well, *I* am," Joey said. "I'm afraid of practically everything in this place, except Ko and you guys. Like that two-headed whatever, and those things in the trees that almost got me, and that *jalla*-something in the water—"

Touriq laughed. "A brook-*jalla*? How can you be afraid of a silly little brook-*jalla*?" He looked around quickly, nudged her with his shoulder and said, "Come on, I'll show you."

THE REST OF THE YOUNG UNICORNS had fallen to grazing or to sparring with their horns, mostly in play, as she had seen them do before. Others were lying in the sun, eyes open—most, like Touriq's, betraying the earliest signs of coming blindness—motionless, entering perfectly into stillness, until even the music of their being fell silent. Joey turned to follow Touriq, and suddenly noticed that one of the unicorns was watching her.

He was white, as white as daisies, and his horn flashed fire in the sun, but it was his own particular eyes that stopped Joey where she stood. They were clear, undimmed, and they were Indigo's eyes. She took a step toward him, but he moved away and vanished among the others, so completely gone that she could not be sure of having seen him at all.

Touriq guided her higher into the hills, along a shadowed path toward the sound of running water. The brook was dark in the shade, and there were red leaves floating on it, and one blue feather. Touriq went to the brink and gave a low, quavering call three times. Nothing happened. He called once more.

A sudden swirl at his feet, a splash, and a brook-*jalla* was there, resting on her elbows halfway up the bank, laughing at them with thin, sharp teeth. "My," she said. "One of the Eldest and an Outworlder, what wonder." She was smaller than Joey, the size of a ten-year-old; she was naked, and her skin had a blue-green glimmer in the dappled sunlight. In a round, child-like face the diamond-shaped eyes that met Joey's—*the same color as her skin*—glowed with an adult mischief. Joey had expected her to have a mermaid's tail, but could not tell if it was so. There was a glint like soap bubbles to the brook-*jalla*'s hands, and Joey realized that her long fingers were delicately webbed.

"What wonder," the brook-*jalla* said again. "I've never seen an Outworlder. Come closer, child."

Joey glanced at Touriq, then walked to the water's pebbly edge and squatted down to be on a level with the diamond eyes. She said, "My name's Joey."

The brook-*jalla* made a sound like John Papas's gold coins sliding together. "That is *my* name," she replied, and laughed again when Joey attempted to mimic it. She said, "Come and swim with me. I will teach you to catch little spotted fish."

Joey shook her head quickly, and was surprised to see the brook-*jalla* lower her strange eyes. "I would not hurt you," she said. "We *jallas* have much need of the company of our own kind, but I am the only one in all the length of this stream. I grow lonely."

"I'm sorry," Joey said. "That's really sad. Can't you just move to another creek, brook, whatever?"

"We live and die where we are born," the brook-*jalla* answered her. "I find companions as I can—birds, water snakes, Old Ones even—but none will swim with me, and I cannot walk in their woods." She raised, not a tail, but a foot out of the water, and Joey saw that it was tiny, three-toed, poignantly useless. The brook-*jalla* said, "For us, that is closeness, the swimming." She reached out and put her webbed hand on Joey's, so lightly that it felt like the kiss of a soap bubble.

Joey looked at Touriq again. The unicorn colt gave no sign to advise her. *Ko said they were harmless. It's the other ones that eat you. I think.* She began taking her clothes off.

The water was just as cold as she had thought it would be, dropping off sharply a little way from the bank. Joey went under, came up gasping and looked quickly around for the brook-*jalla*. There was no trace of her, until a webbed hand clutched Joey's ankle to draw her down again. For an instant she panicked, kicking out, flailing the water—*God, she's strong!*— but the hand immediately released its hold, and the brook-*jalla* was beside her, the diamond eyes gleaming with delight. "Yes," she cried. "This is how we play. Now you."

Joey started to say, "Now me *what?*" but the brook-*jalla* had disappeared again. In her mind Touriq, watching from the bank, called excitedly, "Chase her! Go on!" Joey scanned the surface, spied a trail of dainty silver bubbles just beyond her reach, and plunged.

The brook-*jalla* flashed to meet her, all gristle and sinew and sleek, almost-scaly skin. She never quite extended herself to escape, but twisted and tumbled through Joey's arms, gurgling and purring happily, sometimes turning in a swift, irresistible flurry to trap Joey in her own grip and drag her to the bottom. She could stay under far longer than Joey could, but she always let go at the smallest signal, and was always careful to contain her strength and quickness within Joey's limits. They splashed and laughed and yelped ceaselessly together, except in the silent moments when they sought each other underwater; and Touriq watched from the bank, browsing now and then on the thick yellow moss that grew between the stones.

Joey had no notion of how long she swam with the brook-*jalla*. She stopped only when she was too exhausted for more play, and simply flopped down in the shallows to rest. The brook-*jalla* lay beside her, smiling, not even breathing hard, reaching to touch first Joey's breast and then her own. "Now we are sisters," she said.

Joey blinked. "We are? That's good. I always wanted a sister, and all I've got is this dorky little brother, his name's Scott—"

"Sisters, you and I," the brook-*jalla* repeated. "If you have need, you will come here and call."

"All right, I will," Joey answered. "And if you need me—" She stopped, remembering the brook-*jalla's* feet. "Well, we're sisters," she said. "I'll just know."

"Yes," the brook-*jalla* said. "Goodbye." She touched Joey and herself once again, then shrugged back into deeper water and sank from sight without a ripple. Joey sat looking at the water for a long time.

Dressed, still shaking her hair dry, she walked beside Touriq down from the hills. They were nearing the plain where the unicorns had raced, when Joey saw the white unicorn just ahead of them, standing in the shadow of a great boulder. Even at that distance she knew his eyes.

"Indigo!" she shouted. "Indigo, wait!" The white unicorn hesitated, even took a pace forward, but then wheeled and was out of sight in two bounds. Joey started to call after him again, but did not. She put her arm around Touriq's neck and said, "Boy, one thing about this Shei'rah. People *disappear* on you."

"I won't," Touriq said earnestly. Joey rested her head against his head.

Chapter Five

She truly meant to go home that same day. Even while Touriq cantered sedately back toward Sundown Wood, she was already planning slightly different stories to tell her family, her teachers, BeeBee Huang, and Abuelita —*oh, could I maybe tell Abuelita what really happened?*—just in case she had actually been missed. But time here slipped past with such hazy artfulness that Joey felt most often as she did on waking early to a dark bedroom, glancing at her clock and realizing with inexpressible delight that she had another hour or two to sleep before school. Those were the best and strangest dreams, the ones that came then; but the alarm always sounded more spiteful on those mornings, and she was always a bit disoriented for the rest of the day. Her time in Shei'rah was like those dawn dreams, with one small place in her listening somewhere for the alarm.

"I know I ought to be homesick," she said to Ko, "but it's really hard to be homesick when you're not sure if you're awake or what." As in dreams, there was no dividing her Shei'rah days into hours, minutes, and seconds. She wandered often in the woods with Ko and others of the *tirujai*. The satyr continued to call her "daughter," and to regard her as his personal charge and student in all things concerning Shei'rah. His numerous cousins—every *tiruja* Joey met seemed to be related to every other, in ways so complicated that even Ko gave up on explaining it all to her—accepted her unhesitatingly in the same manner. She ate and enjoyed the fruits, berries, and tubers that they lived on, and cautiously sampled the black juice they made from anything that happened to be fermenting at the time. The younger ones could grow rowdy under its influence, but Joey quickly came to feel as secure in the presence of any satyr as she did with the unicorns themselves. Ko once said proudly to her, "We *tirujai* are like the Eldest, a little. We see in all directions, forward and back, this way and that, only not so far." He paused, and then added, "Also, we do not live forever. I think this is a good thing. I think so."

Often she spent whole mornings or afternoons with the brook-*jalla*. They swam together, always, and played underwater hide-and-seek, and dozed on the bank in the sunlight; and the water sprite, as she had promised, did indeed teach Joey to catch fish with her bare hands. She found it highly puzzling that Joey did not eat them then and there, as she did, but invariably let them go, to be enthusiastically chased again. What the brook-*jalla* liked best, after swimming, was to tell the long, sleepily tangled tales of great storms, hunts, battles, and feasts that her peaceable folk learn from the river-*jallas*, and to be told stories of the strange, wild world beyond the Border. There was no way for her ever to comprehend the notion of using a computer, of shopping at a mall, or of selling real estate, but she loved to hear about them all the same. She did know about brothers, however, and made several bloodcurdling but intriguing suggestions concerning Scott.

But the best part of Joey's days in Shei'rah were passed in the company of unicorns. She usually slept warm, curled between Touriq and his mother Fireez, whom she learned belonged to the sea-born unicorn tribe known as *ki-lins*. "The Lord Sinti is of the sky folk," Fireez told her, "the *lanau*. The *karkadanns* are the *karkadanns*, all earth and stone. We were not made by the same hand, yet we were given Shei'rah to dwell in as one. And this we have done."

The third unicorn Joey had met with Sinti and Fireez— blue-gray, slender, elegantly tranquil—was the Princess Lisha, daughter of Sinti. She spoke less often than any of the others, even her father, but from the beginning Joey found her the most comforting to be around, though she could never have said why. They often walked in Sundown Wood before dawn, or on nights that smelled too good for sleep. The music of Shei'rah always seemed closer and clearer under starlight, especially with a unicorn for a companion.

Once she said in twilight, "I don't get it. You guys crossing the Border all the time, I mean. If I were a unicorn, boy, I wouldn't stir one foot out of Shei'rah. I mean, just about all we've got in *my* world is smog and movies and people starving on television. And it's so beautiful here, even with two-headed snakes and all, I just don't see why you'd ever bother with us."

The Princess Lisha laughed softly. To Joey the laughter of the Eldest always felt like a small, warm breeze inside her mind.

"Dreams," she said. "There is a legend among us that we of Shei'rah dreamed your world into being. I doubt that this is so, but we Eldest do spend more time thinking of humans and marveling at them than you will ever know. Perhaps Shei'rah is bound to your world merely by our endless fascination with it. I cannot explain it, but it must be so. Why else would we be able to take the forms of human beings and nothing else? *We* are what we are forever, unchanging—you are everything all at once, past and present and future all rioting together. I pity you terribly, I could never bear to be like you, but I wonder and wonder about you."

Joey started to speak, changed her mind three times, and managed at last to mumble, "It's not so awful for you being blind, is it? I mean, you all get around fine—nobody'd ever know, except maybe for that stuff on your eyes."

"Moving from one place to another without bumping into a tree is not everything," the Princess Lisha replied quietly. "It lessens us, living forever among shadows. We are simpler creatures than humans, in some ways. We were meant to *see* the world around us, to see it deeply and closely, not to imagine it, not to eavesdrop on it, not to trace it in our minds. Your folk have learned to live with many kinds of blindness, I think, and still somehow remain yourselves. We are not so fortunate, we Eldest." She was silent for some while before she went on, "But the Lord Sinti is our healer, and he will surely find a way to restore our sight. We can wait."

Imperceptibly, the sky had softened into a moment of pale, translucent green, as it always did just before dawn in Shei'rah. Joey said, "I met this guy—this Eldest, I mean—anyway, his name's Indigo. Do you, like . . . do you know him?"

"I know Indigo." The Princess Lisha looked back at Joey with with blind, jeweled eyes that revealed nothing.

Joey rushed on. "Yeah, well, I don't. I mean, I know he's an Eldest, only I met him in, like, human shape, because he crosses the Border a lot because he's *really* fascinated with my world, and that's absolutely all I do know, except he saved me from those whatevers, *criyaquis*. It's not I *like* him or anything—I just want to say thanks, that's all."

Lisha said slowly, "Indigo does not like to be thanked. Indigo does not like a great many things."

"Tell me about it," Joey said. "As far as I know, the only thing he does like is Woodmont, California, and that's crazy." She hesitated. "Do you ever get that here? I mean, you know, Eldest going crazy or something?"

The Princess Lisha laughed again. "We do not have such a word, but I understand your meaning. No, Indigo is not like that. But he has never been like most of us, either. He has no gift for contentment—there is no ease in him, no peace with anything as it is. I do not know whether this is a good thing, a bad thing or neither, but it makes life in Shei'rah very hard for him."

"Well, I still don't get it," Joey said. "I'd trade with him in a hot minute. I would."

Talking so as they walked, they had passed, unnoticing, beyond Sundown Wood, and were well out onto the plain where the young unicorns sported. Joey had begun to say, "I mean, except for Abuelita, that's my grandmother—" when the dawn sky darkened and the icy chattering began.

Joey clutched the Princess Lisha's mane tightly with both hands to keep herself from collapsing with terror. The *perytons* had the sunrise behind them, edging their swarming mass with red-gold as they swept down. Calm as ever, Lisha turned her head for one brief glance back toward Sundown Wood. Her voice rang in Joey's mind. "We would never reach shelter in time. I must stand and fight it out. Let go of me, little one, but stay close to me. They must be very hungry."

71

The *perytons* looked like deer. They were no larger than household cats, borne on dark, tapering wings like the wings of seabirds, but their bodies were those of common deer, down to the dainty cloven hooves and the males' miniature antlers. The only differences, apart from size, were that they smelled like rotting meat, and that their gentle, soft-lipped mouths were bulging with sharp teeth too big for them. Joey realized as she cowered beside the Princess Lisha that the dreadful chattering call of the perytons was nothing more than their teeth clicking together, forever sharpening themselves against one another.

Lisha reared to meet the onslaught. Her defiant bellow astonished and frightened Joey, who had never yet heard the challenge of an enraged Eldest. Her horn flashed left and right into the vanguard of attackers, scattering them and knocking three out of the sky to lie squirming and gnashing among the wildflowers. The *perytons* veered off in disarray for a moment; then the wound in their ranks closed with muddy precision, and they banked as one, tucked their delicate legs up against their bodies, and came for Joey and the unicorn again.

The next few seconds, or minutes, or hours, always remained to Joey an unending nightmare of gull wings beating wildly against her head, crowded yellow jaws snapping frantically inches from her face, and the terrible tiny death-screams that followed each blazing battle roar of the Princess Lisha. Blind or not, she was carrying the fight to the *perytons*, lunging up at them again and again, while her horn wove a deadly circle of sanctuary around Joey. Each time she struck, often too fast for Joey's eyes to follow, another handful of the flying deer-things fell broken beside her, but there were always more. Lisha seemed utterly tireless, but Joey saw that she was bleeding from a score of small, ugly wounds on her neck, shoulders, and flanks. Joey heard the cool voice saying, "You may have to make for the trees after all, little one. I have never seen them like this."

"I'm not going," Joey sobbed. "No way, I'm not leaving you." A *peryton* slipped past the Princess Lisha's whirling guard and made straight for Joey's eyes. Joey had an instant's vision of its own sweet brown eyes streaked with blood and glazed over with desperate voracity, before the horn split it almost in two and hurled it aside. The unicorn said, "I can keep most of them from you if you go now. Keep your head down and mind your feet. You will only stumble if you look back."

In later times, Joey often wondered whether she would have obeyed and abandoned the Princess Lisha, and drew much comfort from the fact that she had not taken so much as a step toward escape when she heard the shattering bellow behind her. A great *karkadann* burst through the trees of Sundown Wood, and the ground shook under his strides as he came bearing down on the battle. His red sides flamed in the morning sunlight, there was foam on his mouth, and in his own overwhelming blindness he looked more like a runaway locomotive than a unicorn.

The *perytons* saw him coming. One being, one awareness, or not, they rose up in a vast swirl of confusion. Half of them seemed to favor retreat, while the others were plainly too ravenous for any counsel but their bellies'. The *karkadann* was in among them while they wavered, towering between them and the Princess Lisha, scything them down pitilessly with a horn twice as long as hers. They endured it for a dreadful moment, then gave in completely and fled wailing across the sky before the two unicorns, who pursued them briefly before halting and turning back. As they trotted toward Joey, they were rubbing affectionately against each other, and Joey saw that the *karkadann*, when not nuzzling and licking Lisha's wounds, was dancing clumsy caracoles around her, kicking up his heels like any baby goat.

"This is Tamirao," the Princess Lisha said almost shyly. The *karkadann* lowered his head before Joey, touching her shoulder lightly with the huge horn. His eyes were the color of lilacs.

JOEY'S WRISTWATCH HAD STOPPED when she crossed the border, and although she quickly learned to guess the hour fairly accurately by the position of the sun or moon, or the taste of the air, the knack ceased to matter to her even more quickly. She ate fruit and berries when she was hungry, slept on soft grass when she was tired, played with Touriq and his friends as she chose, took shelter in the satyrs' dens when it rained, and taught the brook-*jalla* to sing "Yellow Submarine." Sometimes she sat under a tree for an entire day or night, as still as one of the Eldest, listening to the music of Shei'rah. She no longer attempted to draw nearer to it, or to understand its true relationship to the unicorns who were somehow its source. She simply sat listening, all day, humming softly to herself.

Perhaps best of all, she liked watching the Princess Lisha and Tamirao together. The mighty *karkadann* was a silent, lumbering creature, like all his kind, but his devotion to Lisha made him almost as calmly graceful as she, to Joey's eyes. When she saw them strolling in Sundown Wood in the evenings, or watching a dawn-reddened waterfall pounce down a cliffside almost to their feet, she warmed with the reflected joy of it. Lisha often invited her to walk with them, but Joey was always too shy to accept.

The Lord Sinti she met invariably when she least expected to. She never heard or saw him until he was walking at her side, sometimes friendly and—for Sinti—conversational; at others, so faraway, so separate, so still, that she felt foolish and a little frightened, unable to imagine why he might seek her company. Yet there were moments when she suddenly heard him in her mind, though he was nowhere in sight, warning her against a nearing swarm of *perytons* or a rogue *jakhao* strayed into Sundown Wood. Once, stretched out on her belly at a little, shadowy pond, where she liked to chew clover stems and drink the cold, clear water and think of absolutely nothing, she saw his wind-rumpled reflection beside her face, and was certain she heard him say, "Help me, Josephine Rivera." But when she sat up and turned, only the music of his passage remained.

She saw Indigo from afar several times, always in unicorn form, but had only one chance to speak. Ko had taken her, not long after her arrival in Shei'rah, to a mountain valley, austere to the point of barrenness, with which Joey had promptly fallen in love. The climb was a steep one, but she made it often, to sit among a certain jumble of huge stones, which formed a surprisingly comfortable armchair, and gaze down on the backs of smoke-colored birds like winged fish that hovered in one place for hours at a time. In the constant richness of Shei'rah, it contented her deeply to have a place where there was nothing but sky and stone to look at, except for a river glittering far below. Ko warned her repeatedly to stay away from it because of the lurking river-*jallas*, and Joey had faithfully heeded him until the afternoon when she saw the white Eldest at the water's edge.

She was scrambling down the rocks on the instant, skinning her hands and knees and paying no mind to that at all. The distance was far too great for her to distinguish one white unicorn from another, but she told herself wryly as she descended,

"Well, if it's him I'll know, because he'll be out of here the moment he sees me. That's how you tell with Indigo."

It was Indigo, but he did not run. He stood staring into the swift-flowing river, narrow still at this height but already deep and oddly dark, even in direct sunlight. Joey, moving diffidently toward him, came to a complete halt when the sleek golden head and high-boned shoulders rose out of an eddy near the bank. The river-*jalla's* face was shockingly lovely, her huge eyes, butterfly-velvet skin, and wide, tender mouth so perfectly made that Joey put her hands to her own face in awe. She heard Indigo speaking, and then the answering voice, rippling low and amused and sweetly ravenous across the water. The river-*jalla* turned her head and looked at Joey.

Their glances touched for seconds only before Joey had to shut her eyes against what she saw, then and forever after, in the eyes of the river-*jalla*. She heard the enchanting laughter again, and Indigo's voice, suddenly turned commanding; and she opened her eyes in time to see the last mocking flash of a fish-toothed smile as the river-*jalla* slipped from sight, leaving not a ripple to mark her passage. Joey stood where she was and simply shook, until Indigo said without looking at her, "She will not return today. Come here."

Up close, his long-legged slenderness and comparatively coarse coat marked him as one of the *lanau*, the sky-born unicorns, like Sinti and the Princess Lisha. Joey approached slowly, keeping him between herself and the river bank, just in case. She said, "That was the most beautiful woman I've ever seen. I was never so scared in my entire life."

Indigo did not answer. Joey said, "By the way. Thank you for saving my life."

"I have just done it again," Indigo replied. "A river-*jalla* is very much quicker on land than your little brook-*jalla* friend. Tell me, does Ko realize just how stupid you are?"

Joey blazed up instantly. "I know not to go near a river! I only came down here because I wanted to talk to you! What is your problem with me?"

"You do not belong here." Indigo's voice remained tonelessly unyielding in her mind. "You have no business at all in Shei'rah."

"Oh, right, like you belong in my world?" Joey was shouting now as she might have at her brother. "So what the hell are you doing running around in Woodmont, California, trying to sell your horn for gold?" She caught herself, hearing her own words. "Oh, it *was*," she whispered slowly. "That really was your horn you showed Mr. Papas."

Indigo wheeled abruptly away from the river and began walking back toward the stony hills, with Joey yapping at his cloven heels. "It was yours, wasn't it? Unicorns don't die, so it had to be your horn. Am I right? I know I'm right."

The white unicorn led her on until she had literally brought him to bay against a boulder twice Joey's height. He could have vaulted it easily, leaving her to toil hopelessly after him; instead he turned back to face her, the deep blue eyes huge with defiance. "What if it was?"

Joey stared at him. "But you *can't* do that! You can't cross the Border without your horn, and if you can't ever get back to Shei'rah you'll die! Sinti told me!"

"Ah, of course," Indigo said. "The learned Lord Sinti, master of us all, guide and counselor to Outworlders. Sinti the noble, the all-wise, the mysterious. Sinti the liar."

"What are you talking about?" Joey had meant this to be an utterly scornful sneer, but something in Indigo's manner made it come out hoarse and stammering. "Sinti's no liar!"

"Sinti and the rest of them," Indigo said flatly. "Fireez, Lisha, all the great Eldest. Liars all."

"Right," Joey said. "Right." She was determined to keep herself under control. "Let's talk about lying. Like you telling Mr. Papas you had to have gold because you travel all over. You're a unicorn, you live in Shei'rah—what do you need with gold, with going places? I mean, for God's sake, you're already *here!*"

Indigo stared back at her for a long moment, during which Joey became absurdly aware that he smelled exactly like a perfumed bath soap in the shape of a fish that she had loved when she was little. Then he reared, so suddenly that she jumped back in alarm, and this time he did leap the boulder, his hooves barely brushing the top with a sound as soft as the crackle of hair being brushed. Joey did not try to follow. She climbed slowly and sweatily back to her stone chair and sat watching the river for a long time, wondering if the river-*jalla* would show herself again, and half afraid that she would.

The little dragon-like creatures, the *shendi*, fascinated her unceasingly, and she spent a good deal of time lying in tall grass, observing one particular family that inhabited a shallow cave not far from the place where she had seen the two-headed *jakhao*. The parents either ignored her or ran at her, making furious teakettle sounds; but the kits were as curious as she, and early one morning Joey, barely breathing, had lured one close enough to determine that its narrow, horny lips were as green as grass and the pupils of its eyes white-gold, when a rustle behind her sent it scuttling back to the miniature shadow of its mother.

Turning in annoyance rather than fear, she saw Ko.

"It is time," the satyr said. Joey blinked, uncomprehending.

Ko said, "If you stay any longer in this world, time will have passed in your own. The Lord Sinti has directed me to guide you to the Border."

"Oh. Right. Yeah." Joey looked aimlessly around, feeling suddenly as disoriented and doubtful as when she had first found herself in Shei'rah. She said, "I have to say goodbye to a lot of people. The brook-*jalla,* Fireez, Lisha, Touriq, all the Eldest. . . ."

Ko shook his head. "There will not be time. Remember how long a journey it is." Seeing her eyes growing large with unshed tears, he added gently, "Daughter, the Eldest will be with us all the way to the Border, as they watched and followed when you first Crossed. But they do not understand farewells. None of us here do, except perhaps my folk, almost." He took her hand in his own, smiling the careless crooked smile of the *tirujai.* "That is the way that Shei'rah is," he said. "Come now."

The way seemed distinctly shorter than before, even though it was past sunset by the time they dropped down into a narrow, shadowy valley and Joey saw the Border for the first time. In the last light it appeared as a bright, elusive ripple in the air: a kind of trickster mirror that turned all the land beyond it to leering shadows and windblown snow. Joey said, "This isn't where it was. What if I end up in New York or wherever?"

Ko patted her shoulder reassuringly. "That will not happen."

"How do you know? You've never crossed over yourself—how do *you* know where I'm going to come out?" She felt herself suddenly very close to raw panic.

Ko remained unperturbed. "The Border is the Border. You will emerge where you entered, daughter. The Lord Sinti's word on it."

"Well," Joey said. "If *Sinti* says so." She accentuated the black unicorn's name pointedly, saw the swift hurt on Ko's shaggy face, hidden just as swiftly, and stumbled to hug him. "I'm sorry, I'm sorry," she muttered. "I just feel so . . . I don't know, I don't feel good, I hate this."

The satyr's hair smelled unwashed and gamy and wonderful. He said, "Come back, then. The Border will be there. Shei'rah will be there still. Come back to us when you choose."

"But it *moves*," Joey sniffed. "Sinti told me, Shei'rah *moves* all the time. I'll probably never find it ever again."

Ko held her a little away and winked solemnly at her. "I think, daughter—mind you, I say I think—that Shei'rah will wait for you a while. We will see each other soon." He pointed up at a drowsy full moon, just now floating clear of the trees. "*That* will not wait, however. Go now." He embraced her once again, then turned her around, gripped her shoulders, and gave her a slight push toward the misty radiance dividing the world of unicorns, satyrs, and six-inch dragons from the world to which she belonged. Joey rubbed her eyes, started to look back, didn't, heard one last impudent, heartbreaking flirt of the beloved music, silent since she and Ko had set out for the Border, and began walking down the slope in the hiking boots that now felt like iron manacles, trudging wearily but without hesitation straight through the tingling shimmer. . . .

. . . and almost straight into a corner mailbox at Alomar and Valencia, two blocks from her house. She hung onto it, dizzy and disoriented, gaping blankly around her. The night was as dark as when she had run down this street after the music, and the same half-moon—not the moon of Shei'rah—hung low in the east. Joey shook her head repeatedly, swallowing hard, waiting to see if she were going to be sick, and hiding her face against the mailbox in case anyone passing might have seen her come lurching out of empty air. At last she took a long breath, stood up shakily straight, and turned to start home.

No one awoke in her house when she tiptoed up the stairs. She fell on the bed, still wearing her *Northern Exposure* shirt, and dreamed of tiny dragons and of the brook-*jalla's* diamond-shaped eyes.

Chapter Six

The only person she told was John Papas. She was in the shop late the next afternoon, carefully sorting a carton of new violin strings, as he had taught her to do, when she looked up and saw him standing slump-shouldered near the window, looking out at the street. "Dumb," he muttered, far more to himself than to her. "Lost it sure, dumb Papas."

Joey started to say, "He'll be back," but caught herself. On a sudden impulse, she put down the violin strings and walked over to one of the few electronic pianos John Papas kept in stock. She said, "Mr. Papas, listen a minute," and began slowly picking out from memory one of the melodies she heard most often at nightfall in Sundown Wood.

It was a limping, impromptu arrangement she played, embarrassingly skimpy in the left hand, since she could only guess at what Woodmont harmonies might suit the airs and rhythms of Shei'rah. She was improvising much of the time, her hands doggedly lumbering after the music her heart remembered. *It's*

83

all wrong, wrong, it's garbage, you ought to be ashamed. Even so, the clumsy pursuit took her over so completely that, as before, she had no notion of how long she had been playing. She only stopped when she opened her eyes and saw John Papas crying silently.

Adult tears embarrassed Joey greatly. She got up hurriedly and started back to her work. John Papas said thickly, "Leave the strings, leave. Is time to start writing your stuff down, kiddo. Don't know where you get it, but we got to start writing it down. This is what, Friday, you come in tomorrow, I got no repair jobs. . . ."

"It's not my stuff, Mr. Papas," Joey said. "I mean, maybe it is, some way, maybe part of it's mine. But it's like the music that boy Indigo was playing, when he wanted to sell you that horn." John Papas's face turned expressionless, and strangely wary. Joey said, "It's from this other place—this other world, actually, is what it is. It's a place called Shei'rah."

John Papas listened to what she told him without once interrupting her or changing his demeanor. When she had finished, he grunted and turned away to study an ancient valve trombone that had come in for repairs that morning. Over his shoulder he remarked, "Some big-budget dreams you got there, Josephine Angelina Rivera. Cast of thousands, all those special effects, who's your director? You tell me when the movie comes out, all right?"

Joey had never imagined that John Papas would immediately accept her account of unicorns, satyrs, and carnivorous flying deer at face value, but neither had she expected dismissal this casual and derisive. Indignantly raising her voice, she said, "It wasn't a dream! You think I don't know when I've had a dream? I was there for days, weeks—I was *there!*"

John Papas muttered something she could not make out, bending over the trombone with his back to her. A surge of anger took Joey over completely then, and she shouted at him, "And you know it's true! You know where that music comes from, because you knew Indigo! I could tell right away you knew him!"

John Papas turned slowly to face her. He was very pale, which made his black eyes look bigger than they were, and the skin just under his left eye was twitching visibly. He said quietly, "I met him at the Border."

The sudden admission left Joey all but speechless. "The Border," she stammered. "You crossed the Border, you've been there? You've *been* to Shei'rah?"

John Papas shook his head, actually smiling a small smile. "No. Was an accident. I found your Border—you want to know where I found it? Down the block, right across the street from Provotakis's dump. Right across the street, one night, maybe a year ago. The Border."

"It moves around," Joey said. "I never even noticed it, not exactly. I was just chasing the music."

"Chasing the music." John Papas's smile broadened slightly, though the grimace seemed painful to him. "Me, I didn't hear no music. You play it, *he* plays, then I hear fine. Otherwise I can't hear it, not across the street, not across the Border." He snorted harshly and pulled at his mustache. "So. So I'd been drinking *ouzo* with Provotakis, we do that sometimes. Drink, talk about things. So he closes up, it's one, two in the morning, I'm full of *ouzo*, I come outside, there it is. There it is. Right in my face, practically, looks like—what?—like rain. Like some kind of electric rain."

Joey said, "But you didn't cross?"

"I'm not a kid," John Papas said. "Just a drunk old man. I stand and I look, that's all. I try to understand what it is I'm seeing. Only I can't see to the other side, not quite. And then. Then the white unicorn."

"Indigo," Joey breathed. John Papas did not seem to have heard her. He said, "White like salt, white like bone. Standing right on the Border, front feet click-click in a Woodmont street, back feet—back feet, who knows where? And he looks at me. You know what that's like, when he looks at you."

"I know," Joey said. "I know."

"He saw me," John Papas said. "Me, I'm still not sure if I saw *him*, but he saw me. And we talk." He laughed suddenly, genuinely. "Me, old Papas, one too many *ouzos*, talking all night to a white unicorn. What do you think about that, Josephine Angelina Rivera?"

"What did you talk about?" Joey demanded. "What did it tell you, the unicorn?"

John Papas spread his hands. "Asked, mostly. All night long, asking questions about this world—people, countries, languages, history, money. Oh yeah, especially money." He rubbed his forehead and winced, remembering. "Wake up next morning, my head's killing me, I think it was a dream. A unicorn in L.A., *ouzo* gives you that kind of dream, you know? And then *he* walks into the store. On two feet he walks in, but I knew."

His eyes were suddenly full of tears again, but at the same time his head was wagging in helpless comedy. "He wants to live here, you believe that? Wants to cross over for good, look human, live human, sell the horn, the hell with this unicorn business. You believe that?"

"He can't," Joey said. "He can't, it won't work. He'll die." John Papas looked back at her. Joey said, "An Eldest, a unicorn who loses his horn can't get back to Shei'rah. He'll die here. He knows that."

"Well, you better remind him," John Papas said quietly. He nodded over Joey's shoulder, and she turned to see Indigo entering the shop, holding the silver-blue horn carelessly in one hand. Even knowing what he was, she still marveled at the unhuman grace of the way he moved—*no, not unhuman— more like he's so proud he can take this shape that he's doing it the absolute best he can. We're the ones who don't look human, next to him.*

"I thought you might want to see the horn again," Indigo said. He held it out for John Papas's inspection. John Papas reached for it; then made a wry, bitter grimace and let his hand drop to his side. He said, "What difference? I got no more gold than I had last time."

Without answering, Indigo lifted the horn to his mouth. The quick, small scamper of notes tumbled through the shop, *there, with love from Shei'rah.* He stopped abruptly and handed the horn to John Papas.

John Papas held the horn as though he were holding a child. Indigo watched him, smiling thinly. Neither of them spoke. John Papas looked at Indigo for a moment, and then walked away toward his workshop. Joey said, "You'll die without it. Sinti told me."

"And what did I tell you about the Lord Sinti? What was the word I used?" Indigo's smile broadened slightly. "There are three Eldest living just in this one town of yours. You see them on the street every day, and you never know."

"You're crazy, " Joey whispered. "Eldest in Woodmont? You're crazy."

Indigo laughed at her, and the sound was almost as elusively playful as his music. "In Woodmont, and wherever else the Border touches your world. You see, I told you, they lie, Sinti and the rest. We can live here and take no harm. We can live well here."

Joey started to shout, "No, I don't believe you," but she suddenly remembered the thoughtful voice of the Princess Lisha, musing, "Perhaps Shei'rah is bound to your world merely by our endless fascination with it." She lowered her own voice, hearing John Papas returning, and simply asked Indigo, "Why? Why would any of you *want* to live here? To look like us? When you could be the Eldest in Shei'rah?"

For a moment, when Indigo looked at her, there was none of the usual easy mockery in his face, nor the beauty of another world either, but something resembling human pain. He said, as quietly as she, "And do you think that is such a wonderful thing? To be eternally magical, angelic, pure, with no choice at all? No say ever in who you are because of *what* you are? I tell you, you stupid, stupid, ignorant, miserable little mortal object, I would rather be you than to be the Lord Sinti himself. And none of the Eldest has ever said such a thing to any creature."

"Well," Joey said. "Well, hurray for you." Angered by Indigo's words, she was nevertheless so dazed by the passion in his voice that she could think of nothing else to say. John Papas came up to them, his eyes weary. He said, "I can maybe find a little more gold. You come back in a few days, a week, we'll see."

"Perhaps," Indigo said. He took the silver-blue horn from John Papas's hands and was gone without another word, though Joey called after him, "Listen, wait, we have to talk!" The door slammed, leaving her and John Papas to blink foolishly at each other, with the music of Shei'rah still somehow laughing in the shop's dusty corners.

88

John Papas said flatly, "I got to have it. Never in my life, there was nothing, nothing I ever got to have like that thing, that horn. I'm ashamed I want like that, tell you the truth."

"I know," Joey said. "I do. But it's crazy, he can't do that, selling his horn. I don't care what he said—if they lose their horns here, the Eldest, they can't ever get back to Shei'rah. He'll die here, Mr. Papas, he knows he'll die here!"

"His business," John Papas said. "His choice. Me, I never crossed no Border, so the only thing *I* know"—and he reached out abruptly to ruffle her hair—"I got a scraggly little kid hangs around all the time, suddenly she's full of music like I never heard in this world, like nobody ever heard. But they will. Jesus and all the saints, they will."

Joey tried to interrupt him, but he was unstoppable, dreaming aloud as she had never seen him do. "Okay, main thing, you got to learn to write the music down real fast now, you got to learn how to weave the voices together, how to paint with the voices, you understand me? You got to make it so people *see* that place you go to, Shei'rah, so they *feel* it, not just hear. Lot of hard work ahead, Josephine Angelina Rivera." He prodded her gently toward the piano again.

"I can't," Joey said. Her mouth was dry and her throat hurt. She said, "I have to go, I'll see you tomorrow." And she was outside, blind for a moment in the white sun, then running back along the street, sweating and panicky, bumping into people, staring into every face she passed for old eyes out of Shei'rah.

TO HER OWN SURPRISE, she caught up with Indigo in two blocks. He was walking slowly, for once, moving as smoothly as always, but his shoulders seemed a little slack, his head and neck less arrogantly poised. He carried the silver-blue horn tucked under his arm.

Joey fell into step beside him, catching her breath. As soon as she could speak, she demanded, "Okay, show me." Indigo glanced at her and looked away. Joey said, "Eldest. Where are they? Show me just one."

Indigo began to walk faster. "Why should I? I have other things to do."

Joey laughed. "You know what Abuelita, my grandmother, you know what she says about people like you? She says you're all feathers." Indigo halted and turned to face her. Joey smiled at him. "No bird," she said. "Just feathers."

For a moment it seemed to her that Indigo looked oddly weary and almost sad as he stared at her. Three girls pushed by them in the slow twilight, looking sideways; an ice-cream truck came down the street playing "The Entertainer." Indigo's blue eyes filled with mockery once again, from some deep, limitless source, and he said, "Why not? After all, why not? Come with me."

She had to hurry to keep up with him, but he was not trying to lose her; indeed, whenever they crossed a vast parking lot or moved through a busy mall, he would take her arm to keep them from being separated. They were heading into the business district, where Woodmont blurred into another suburb on the far side of the freeway, and where shopping would go on until nine or ten o'clock. Indigo led her unfailingly into whatever neonlit storefront or arcade was playing even louder, uglier music than the last. Watching him scanning the crowds, his quick, cocked head never still, she thought, *He loves it, all of it, he loves anything that isn't Shei'rah. I'm never going to understand.*

"When she is here she sits *there*," he said suddenly, nodding toward the entrance of Mex to the Max Tacos. "But I think she has already gone back to the place where she sleeps. Come."

The freeway passed above all but the tallest Woodmont buildings, but its off-ramp spilled almost directly into the downtown area. Indigo's hand was painfully tight on Joey's wrist as he pulled her into the hot dusk between the pillars. Strangely, it was less noisy than she had imagined, as though the darkness muffled the hollow roar of the road overhead. Indigo said, "This way."

Joey trotted after him over the cracked pavement, sidestepping stagnant puddles and mounds of garbage, but getting oil stains on her shoes anyway. Figures passed them or fled from them in the dimness, pushing clattering shopping carts, hugging great slabs of cardboard under their arms, or struggling with overfilled green plastic bags like forlorn Santa Clauses. No one spoke to Joey and Indigo, even to ask for spare change. Some of the women looked directly at them, but the men never did.

She had been hearing the music of Shei'rah for some moments before she truly heard it, in that setting. It sounded as injured as the eyes of the people under the freeway, fluttering up momentarily on a single horn from somewhere ahead, only to limp again, but it was Shei'rah even so, making itself known. Joey stood still.

Indigo beckoned impatiently. "Come. Did you not want to see an Eldest living in your world, your city, your time? Here she is then, come on." He walked on without looking back, and after a moment Joey followed him.

The woman was sitting on a heap of old newspapers with her back against a pillar, playing a scarlet horn almost half her own size. Her layers of clothing were the color of dead skin. She had heavy, dirty red hair, a lean face with a knobby chin and pale eyes that slanted down at their outer corners. But her smile, when she recognized Indigo, was warm with the unmistakable light of the Border itself, and when she raised the horn like a royal trumpeter, for an instant the music of Shei'rah pierced Joey's heart beyond any expecting, any readiness, as it always did. But it broke off quickly, fraying and unraveling, wandering away like water over ground too dry to take it in. The woman shrugged, seemingly unconcerned.

"Oh, my God," Joey said softly. She pushed by Indigo and stood before the woman, demanding, "What are you doing here? You don't *belong* here. You have to get back to Shei'rah."

The woman's pale eyes—puffy, tinged with red, but still as painfully clear as the sky over Shei'rah—regarded her with a chilling tranquility. "I like it here," she said. She reached down for a grubby styrofoam cup and held it out, shaking the few coins together as John Papas had shaken his wooden box.

Joey barely restrained herself from clutching at the woman's high, thin shoulders. "What are you talking about? You can't *like* it, begging on the street, playing *that* music for pennies! You remember Shei'rah, I know it, I know you do! Over there you're on top, you're like a princess, it's your world. What are you *doing?*"

The woman only nodded sleepily past her at Indigo, who moved up beside Joey and dropped down into a crouch, his eyes plainly seeing nothing but her eyes. "I like it here too," he said very softly to her. "Hello, Valadyi."

"Indigo," the woman murmured. She lowered the horn and peered at him as intensely as he was regarding her. Joey backed away, feeling invisible and shut out. One foot skidded in something she knew better than to look at, and she scraped it angrily on the pavement, which felt as faraway as Shei'rah. Indigo was saying something that Joey could not hear, but his voice sounded astonishingly tender. The woman laughed in response and said clearly, "No, it's nice here. This is nice."

Something bumped hard into Joey from behind, almost knocking her over. A stocky, balding black man with a patchy gray beard shoved his PayLess Drugs cart between her and Indigo, who stepped back quickly. "Got you something," he told the woman in a voice that creaked with asthma. He dug between nameless things in the cart until a greasy white bag surfaced. "Slice of pizza and a diet Fresca. Here, go."

The woman smiled slowly and took the bag from him. She offered him a bite of the congealing pizza, but he shook his head, wheezing, "No, baby, that's for you. You go 'head, eat it up." He unfolded a newspaper beside her, sat down on it carefully, laid a heavy arm across the woman's shoulders, and only then allowed his eyes to focus on Indigo and Joey. "This my lady," he said firmly. "We together."

"Yes," Indigo said with great gentleness. "Yes, I see you are." He made an small gesture of farewell, touching his forehead where the horn would have been. The woman lifted her own scarlet horn lazily and saluted him with a swift soap-bubble fanfare out of Shei'rah. Indigo turned and walked away.

Joey was already walking fast with her head down, as though she were marching into the wind, and it was Indigo's turn to hurry after her. She did not speak until they had passed the off-ramp and turned away from the freeway. Then she said, "That was *horrible*. Sitting there in trash, living on pizza—an Eldest! That is the creepiest, the worst thing I ever saw in my *life*."

"How interesting." Indigo's voice was dry, but not at all derisive. "Now I am an Eldest, and much older than you, and that was truly the most beautiful thing I ever saw. And you will never understand that."

"No," Joey said. "Not ever." She kept walking without once looking up, and so she never knew when Indigo left her.

Chapter Seven

On the first Sunday after her return, she took two buses to visit Abuelita at the Silver Pines Guest and Rest Home, as she did every Sunday, whether her family came with her or not. Abuelita was downstairs to meet her, waiting on the hard little bench near the front door where residents were supposed to meet their visitors. She was wearing a frayed old flowered dress that Joey had loved since childhood, ancient straw sandals, and the black wool *reboso* that she wore in all weather around her shoulders. Her broad Indian nose came to Joey's chin when they hugged each other.

The fluffy blonde receptionist—*la bizcocha rubia*, Abuelita called her—cooed over them as she always did when they signed out together. "So *sweet*, everybody says so! And now we're off on our little weekly jaunt, are we? Just so *cute*."

In the grave, precise English that she could still speak when she bothered to, Abuelita replied, "No. *I* am going for a walk with my granddaughter Josefina. *You* are going to stay here and pray that no one dies before your lunch hour. Come,

'Fina." She winked at Joey as she turned away, but the movement itself was like a door closing.

"I skipped my nap," she went on in Spanish, tucking her arm through Joey's. "They don't like it when we miss our naps. I think that is the time when they get to fool around with each other." Behind them *la bizcocha rubia* was saying over and over, louder and louder, to a smudgy-eyed old man in a bathrobe, "Mr. Gerber, you can't find her because she's been in the hospital for a two weeks. She's in the *hospital,* Mr. Gerber!"

Abuelita said calmly to Joey, "His wife is dead. The other woman, the one who is supposed to tell us these things is on vacation. She will tell him next week, when she gets back."

"I hate this place," Joey said. "I hate the food, I hate the *smell*—it smells like a hospital, only they aren't even trying to make people well, just quiet. I wish you'd just come and live with us again."

Abuelita put an arm around Joey's shoulders. "It would never work, 'Fina. I am too old and stubborn and mean to live with anybody, really—probably even your grandfather, if he could come back. And I cannot live alone, I know it, because of the arthritis, and also I fall down sometimes. So for me this place is like any other, no worse, no better. Let's take our walk now, yes?"

Silver Pines was located on a low hill overlooking two freeways and a cemetery. Abuelita found this hilarious; but then Abuelita's sense of humor had always worried her family, except for Joey. The two of them walked arm in arm, chatting comfortably in Spanish, around the swimming pool towards the golf course which was the main social feature of the nursing home. Just beyond it lay a small, carefully landscaped park where residents were encouraged to stroll, and where the weekly

talent shows and *tai-chi* classes were sometimes held. Joey and Abuelita, walking slowly, could circle the entire park in eleven minutes. They usually did it three times.

It took Joey until well into their second circuit before she managed to ask hesitantly, "Abuelita, do you ever believe in other worlds? Not like planets, I don't mean that. Just other—other *places*, really close by, that you can't see?"

The old woman looked at her in mild surprise. "Of course, 'Fina. That place where Ricardo, your grandfather, where he waits for me, where he watches over us, of course I believe. How not?"

"Well, I wasn't exactly thinking of heaven or anywhere," Joey said. "Not exactly."

Abuelita's chuckle was warm and dark. "Nor was I. I knew your grandfather." She peered more closely into Joey's face. "'Fina, at my age I can believe whatever I want to, for as long as I want to. So maybe yes, maybe I could believe in some other world, maybe a lot of them, who knows? Why do you ask me this?"

Joey drew a deep breath, letting it out in quick little puffs. "Because I . . . because . . . I don't know, Abuelita. Never mind."

Her grandmother stopped walking. "'Fina, what?" She put a stubby-fingered, surprisingly strong hand on Joey's wrist.

"*Gatita, pajarita*, what is it? Tell."

"Because," Joey said. She took another long breath. In sudden English she burst out, "Because there really is another world, another place, whatever, and I've been to it. It's got satyrs and phoenixes and two-headed snakes, and it's got unicorns, Abuelita, only they call themselves the Eldest, and they make this *music*, it comes out of them, it's like nothing I can even tell you about. And there are people who live in the water, and you can stay a

97

long time, like I did, and nobody here knows you've been gone. And I didn't dream it, Abuelita, and I'm not making it up, I'm really, really not. It's called Shei'rah, and I've been there."

Abuelita raised both hands in mock surrender. "*Socorro, despacio,* slow down, slow down, 'Fina. I'm an old woman, I can't listen as fast as you can talk." She was laughing, but her eyes were still and serious. "Tell me about this, 'Fina. Slowly. In Spanish."

They walked many more times than usual around the little park that day, but neither of them noticed. The last circuit was completed in silence, which was abruptly broken by the sound of a voice calling, "Mrs. Rivera! Mrs. Rivera!" Joey looked up to see one of the attendants from Silver Pines hurrying toward them across the golf course.

"*Mierda!*" Abuelita said. "My checkup, I forgot about it. They are always so anxious to know how long I might need the bed." She waved to the attendant, then turned and took Joey's face gently between her hands. "Listen, 'Fina, I have to think about what you tell me. I just have to think a little. You understand?" Joey nodded. Abuelita said, "This place, this Shei'rah— you didn't happen to see your *Abuelo* Ricardo anywhere? No. Never mind." She waved again and called, "We are coming, *Senorita* Ashleigh! Stop running, you will give yourself a heart attack and they will put you in with me!"

THE DAYS PASSED. Joey went to school, got on well enough with her parents when they were home, quarreled regularly with her brother Scott, slept over occasionally at BeeBee Huang's house, spent several afternoons a week doing odd jobs at Papas Music, and developed a habit of peering intently into the eyes of street musicians, homeless men and women, and the lurching, half-mad beggars who, by city ordinance, did not exist in Woodmont. She met no others of the Eldest, but she never stopped looking for them.

Indigo did not return. John Papas shuffled about the shop, uncharacteristically short-tempered, often disappearing to make mysterious telephone calls, usually long and always in Greek. Frequently he interrupted Joey's usual chores to give her an impromptu music lesson, telling her constantly, "Write, write, you got to get it down, that stuff you hear over there, that place. What's the good of hearing, you can't get it down?" Joey did her best to remember about triads and passing tones, tenths and minor sevenths and the cycle of fifths, but the words and the numbers, the piano keys themselves, seemed to have so little to do with the air she breathed in Shei'rah that she often threw up her hands and stormed out of the shop, slamming the door to make the old panes rattle. But she always came back the next day. There was only one other place for her to go.

And she was afraid to try to go there again. John Papas questioned her more and more as the days went by with no sign of Indigo. "You ever think about seeing maybe you could find that place again, that Border? Just, you know—just to see?"

Joey nodded, turning from arranging music albums. "All the time. Every minute, practically."

John Papas made a point of looking away, mumbling as he straightened the truss rod in a guitar neck, "Well, so, maybe you should try. Couldn't hurt nothing."

"Me," Joey said. "It could hurt me. I pass that street corner anyway twice a day, every day, and each time I think, *okay, today is it, this time I'm really going to walk a block, half a block, and it'll be Shei'rah, Shei'rah and the music, and the Eldest and everybody, right now, right now.* But I never do. Because what if I walked down that street and nothing happened? No music, no Border, no Shei'rah, just nothing. I couldn't stand that, Mr. Papas. I'd rather not know, you know?" She was not crying, but her eyes felt like cold, heavy stones in their sockets.

"Yah," John Papas said. His voice was muffled and expressionless, but he put his hand on her shoulder. "Yah, I know, Josephine Angelina Rivera. But all your life that's just when you got to go find out. Better, believe me. That too I know."

After a moment he added diffidently, "That boy, that Indigo, could be you see him over in that place." Joey looked up at him. John Papas said, "You could tell him, Papas is getting the money together. A little more time, is all I need. You'd remember that?"

"I remember," Joey said. She shrugged away from his hand. "I remember that it's his horn you want, and you don't care about one thing else. Not him, not the music, not me either. Yeah, you ought to be ashamed, Mr. Papas." She worked the rest of that afternoon without speaking to him, and John Papas stayed in his little office until she left.

BUT ON THE VERY NEXT NIGHT, on the night of another half-moon, for all Joey's fears that the Border would have moved just far enough that she would never find it, the pale-silver shiver in the air was exactly where she had emerged from Shei'rah, just beyond the mailbox at Alomar and Valencia. She stood still for a long time, while cars and buses passed and children of her own age whipped by on glittering neon rollerblades, glancing at her with mild scorn. Then she took two steps forward and was laughing and crying in Ko's reeky arms under the mustard-flower sun of Shei'rah.

"How did you *know?*" she demanded, when she could speak. "How could you tell I'd be crossing right here, right this minute? *Touriq*, that *tickles*—" for a horn had brushed gently across her cheek and a warm breath stirred the hair on the back of her neck. The satyr beamed and preened his beard with both grubby hands.

"I felt it here, daughter," he explained proudly. "We know things in our beards, we *tirujai*. Whenever we are in doubt, uncertain, one of us will say, 'Remember, follow your beard,' and we always do, and it always leads us to where we should be." He hugged her again, and stepped aside to let Joey scramble up on the waiting back of the unicorn colt. Touriq uttered a blaring challenge to rival the Princess Lisha's battle shout, rearing in such fierce joy that Joey almost slid to the ground. Ko caught her, crying out, "'Ware my daughter, Eldest! Is this how you welcome the guest of the Lord Sinti, Outland sister of brook-*jallas*? I'll carry her myself if you treat her so."

Touriq hung his head meekly, waited for Joey to right herself on his back, and then paced forward with such an assumed air of gracious deliberateness that Ko burst out laughing as he ran alongside, springing into the air and clicking his cloven hooves together. And that was how Joey came back to Shei'rah, burying her face against the arched neck of a prancing unicorn, and filling her ears with the deep, warmly raucous laughter of a creature half-human and half-goat, who called to her, "Welcome home, daughter! Welcome home!" And the music of Shei'rah leaped and exulted with him.

She never truly learned, neither then nor each time she returned, whether weeks, months or even years passed in Shei'rah during her absences. The closest she ever came to understanding was when the Lord Sinti said to her, "Because Shei'rah touches your world does not mean that both move through the universe at the same pace. Imagine that you are riding your comrade Touriq, and that I am no Eldest but a *kadrush*," referring to a huge, boneless four-footed slug of the Shei'rah hills. "You could speed the world round thirty times before I had trudged the distance between us now. And if then you leaped from Touriq's back to my own—why, how would you feel that you had traveled any distance at all? So it is with Shei'rah and your Woodmont in California." And with that explanation she had to make do.

This second time, the blue leaves had fallen—though never the red leaves of Sundown Wood—and the nights were cool enough that she made mossy nests to sleep in, as the *tirujai* did. So there were seasons in Shei'rah, after all. Touriq and his friends were unchanged to her eye (perhaps they seemed slightly taller, their soft young manes a bit fuller); but the *shendi*, the family of miniature dragons, appeared alarmingly to have shrunk, until Joey realized that these were a new litter, barely a month out of the egg. The *perytons*, on the other hand, looked ominously larger, even from a wary, shuddering distance, having grown their winter coats, as all deer will do. The fearsome two-headed *jakhaos* were gone, sleeping out the chill time in the ancient caves of their birth, Ko told her. Joey noticed a gray patch in the greasy curls on his chest which she could have sworn had not been there before. The satyr insisted that it was nothing but good Shei'rah dirt, so they left it at that.

As for the brook-*jalla*, she remained as constant as the waters of her stream—more so, since they had turned even colder than Joey remembered them, while the brook-*jalla* was as warm as the newly wakened child she resembled. When it was clear to her that Joey had no intention of putting so much as a toe into the water this season, her Shei'rah-sister swarmed up the bank and leaped dripping into her arms, laughing and kissing her as they tumbled on the shore. "How long you were gone! I thought you must be an old, old woman by now!" Joey, so wet that she might as well have been in swimming, started to explain to her about the time difference; but the brook-*jalla* grew bored quickly and wanted to hear more stories about freeways and fish sticks. She had a completely original conception of the latter.

That second stay went by terrifyingly swiftly for someone who never could assume that she would find her way to this place again. Joey divided her time as well as she could between racing and wandering and racing again with Touriq and the other young unicorns, learning the tales and medicines and the old, old secrets of the *tirujai*, and enduring the freezing mountain water of the brook-*jalla*'s stream for the sake of her wild laughter and her wild tenderness. She insisted on helping to wash Joey's few clothes, with which she would race up and downstream, flourishing them like captured banners and pounding them dramatically on stones to clean them. Clothes and dirt were equally fascinating notions to the brook-*jalla*.

The great Eldest she saw not at all. Touriq—who was very proud of spending his first season apart from his mother Fireez—explained that during this time the oldest unicorns retired with the Lord Sinti to a part of Sundown Wood even the *tirujai* did not know. Joey promptly became passionately determined to find it, and prowled Sundown Wood alone for hours, listening to the low talk of the red leaves and the grumbling of strange creatures turning in their deep winter lairs. It was at such times that she heard most clearly, however close or far it might be, the music of Shei'rah.

Once she walked around a bush at dusk and came face to startled face with a pair of birds colored like jays, but larger, with the long legs of a wader and the jaunty crests of California quail. Their feathers seemed to be illuminated from within, casting a starry blue glow all about them as they strutted unhurriedly by her. Ko told her later that they were called *ercines* and that their phosphorescent trail would guide her to safety if she ever should lose her way. But she never feared becoming lost: in Sundown Wood there was no *lost* to be.

The *shendi* rarely showed themselves in this season, the *criyaqui* not at all, and the *perytons* seemed to be hunting elsewhere, for now. She did spend one entire afternoon in a staring match with a cat-faced creature that somehow supported a burly, scaly body on legs that looked as boneless and infinitely supple as garden hose. Communication was limited, because the beast was on the ground and Joey prudently up a tree, though it clearly invited her to come down and visit. She declined, and towards evening it went away, but Joey spent the night in the tree anyway.

"It was no creature of Shei'rah," Ko said when she described it to him. "The Eldest say that there are many and many worlds beyond yours and mine, daughter. If that is so, might there not be other Borders as well?"

"Oh, I don't like that," Joey answered, though she was more indignant by now than frightened. "I hate that. That's too much, it's too scary."

Ko shrugged and sighed, scratching his tangled head and smiling his crooked smile. "Ah, well, we do not think much about such things, we *tirujai*. It makes our heads hurt."

Joey looked at him without speaking for a long time. On a sudden impulse, she asked him, "Ko, how old is a hundred and eighty-seven years? For you guys? I mean, really."

The satyr fidgeted, refusing to meet her eyes. Joey repeated the question. Ko's reply, when it came, was barely audible. "For a *tiruja*, I would be close to your age. Almost the same."

"Well," Joey said. "Well, you *fraud*! Calling me daughter all the time, and you're just a dorky little kid like me, like Touriq. Ko, you total phony!"

"I am older than Touriq," Ko muttered. He looked so forlorn that Joey had to hug him then, and reassure him that he had always given the impression of being vastly older than his years, until he was comforted.

THE CLOSEST SHE EVER came to a sight of the eldest Eldest was a momentary glimpse of two shadows that just might have been the Princess Lisha and her lover, the *karkadann* Tamirao, walking slowly together in the twilight. But it was during that time of searching that she made a discovery that she had not sought and did not at all wish to make. She came across the bones of a unicorn.

It was in the high desert country of Shei'rah: a wind-scoured, cleanly desolate place where Joey went rarely, because of *jakhaos*, and because being there always made her worry too much about Abuelita and feel guilty about not missing the rest of her family more than she did. But the great serpents were safely underground for the season; and Joey had just begun to wonder seriously whether she could possibly draw a map of all Shei'rah, as BeeBee Huang would immediately have set out to do. She was sitting on a petrified tree stump, pensively doodling in the sand with a stick, when she struck something hard and dug barehanded to fetch it up. She took much longer than she should have to make herself understand what she had found.

There was no way of telling which of the Eldest it was who rested there under the sands. Joey sat holding the delicate skull and the long, still-elegant bones for some while; then replaced them as carefully as she could, said a small prayer that her grandmother had taught her, and went away.

She said nothing at all to Ko or Touriq, nor did she allow herself to think very much about the implications of her find. Rather, she spent much of that time in Shei'rah either in the company of the brook-*jalla* or of the *tirujai*, neither having the least interest in the secrets of the Eldest. Both offered warm, unquestioning companionship, and Joey immersed herself in that, even to the point of catching cold from too much time spent learning to swim with an elusive all-over wriggle of her body. She was still feeling fragile on the morning when she felt the Lord Sinti's voice stirring in herself saying, "*It is time*," and Touriq came to guide her to the Border.

She hoped very much to encounter Sinti himself on the journey. She had questions to ask him, and she sensed that the black unicorn might not be faraway. But he did not appear. They had almost reached the Border when Joey turned to speak to Touriq, smelled bath soap, and found that it was Indigo walking by her side. He said, "Your friend dashed off on some idiot errand or other. He will blunder back quickly."

Despite the words, there was none of the usual insolence in his voice. Joey stopped walking. She said, "You guys die."

"We are not immortal," Indigo answered, "only very, very ancient. Nor do we all go off with the Lord Sinti to spend the cold months in deep meditation. Let the spring come, perhaps one or another does not return—then the Eldest say that he has simply left us, withdrawn into the Great Solitude, as we all do sooner or later. That is their first lie. The other you know."

"Why?" Joey whispered. "Why can't they just tell the young ones straight out? Everybody dies."

"Old lies become truth in enough time. This is a very old lie, older than the Lord Sinti himself. When one grows old enough, one joins the lie. Is it so different on your side of the Border?" Joey did not reply. Indigo said, "How it began, I do not know. What I do know is that I will not be part of it."

"Uh-huh," Joey said. "So you're coming over to live an honest life on my side of the Border. *Dumb.*"

"You have met another of the Eldest who feels just as I do." For the first time, Indigo sounded defensive. "There are many more."

"Well, if they're all living like that one, I'd say you've got a problem." Joey's tone, in her own ears, was as contemptuous as Indigo's had ever been, and she made a hopeless effort to soften it. "I just think it's just so *dumb*, and I wish you wouldn't do it, that's all."

"It is foolish," Indigo said quietly. "Of course it is foolish, and there will never be more than a few of us who make that choice. But it is our choice, the first one any of us ever made. Do not try to imagine what even a foolish choice is like for a unicorn. You never can, Outworlder."

Impulsively Joey put her hands on his face, as Abuelita had held her. She said, "Indigo, that woman under the freeway, she still had her horn. I bet those others do too. I bet there's never been an Eldest who sold his horn." Indigo backed away sharply, tossing his head. Joey said, "You want to sell yours, so you'll have the money to live better than they do. But they'll be the ones who make it, who live, and you'll die. The Lord Sinti told the truth about that. You'll die, Indigo."

She could barely hear the white unicorn's reply. "But I will live! *I will live!*"

He was gone then, and a moment later Touriq was back,

gripping a clump of soggy-looking bulbs in his teeth. "These are for you—*mormarek*, we call them. They are past their best, a little, but when you eat them you can think of me, and my mother, and Ko, and Shei'rah." When Joey hugged his neck in farewell, the unicorn colt whispered, "Come back soon. I miss you." No one but Abuelita had ever said that to Joey in her life, and she crossed the Border in tears. It would not be for the last time.

Chapter Eight

School ended. Joey's brother Scott went off to soccer camp, and her parents left for their annual two weeks in the San Francisco Bay area with Mrs. Rivera's family. Joey was allowed, after much pleading and conniving, to stay with BeeBee Huang, but she spent every free moment at Papas Music, trying to learn to transcribe the music of Shei'rah on the piano. Her frantic impatience made the task far more difficult than it might have been otherwise: she caught onto the language of musical notation quickly enough, but turning the blue trees and tiny dragons of Shei'rah into black squiggles on a smudged sheet of staff paper drove her into fits and tantrums of frustration. "Why can't *you* do it?" she wailed at John Papas over and over. "I'll play, you can just tape it, copy it when you've got ten minutes. Why do I have to be the one doing all the writing?"

"Because you're the one hears the music," John Papas would answer her, implacably calm—in this matter he refused to lose patience with her. "Because you're special. Me, I don't hear the music like you do—maybe I used to, but I don't no more, that's why I can't play it. Because it's a sin, practically, you let somebody else write down what you feel, what you hear. That's a sin, you could lose being special, wind up selling used banjos, like me. Come on, pay attention, you call that a barline? Wobbles like me coming out of Provotakis's place. And how many times I got to tell you, the little flags always go on the right—half-note, quarter-note, sixteenth, don't matter. Come *on.*"

So he coaxed her, teased her, cajoled her, drove her on until at surprising last she began to see Fireez looking back at her through the grubby prison bars of the staff lines, and to feel the laughter of the brook-*jalla* in her fingers when she scribbled a flurry of grace notes. *I might be getting it, Shei'rah. Abuelita, I really might be getting it right.*

When she ventured to say this to John Papas, he looked at her for a long time before he answered, his voice surprisingly gentle. "Nah, it's never *right*, Josephine Angelina Rivera. This world, that world, doesn't matter. You never make people to see what you see, hear, feel what you feel. Notes don't do it, words don't do it, paints, bronze, marble, nothing. All you can do, you maybe get it a little close, a little closer. But *right*, like you're talking? No. No."

She went to Shei'rah when she chose, often crossing the Border three or four days in a row. At other times, aware of her growing addiction to the world of the Eldest, and frightened of it, she would force herself to stay away for an entire week. The Border had apparently settled on Alomar and Valencia—a dark, narrow street barely more than an alley—as its earthly coordinates, for the time being; but each time Joey stepped across it, her foot came down in a different place in Shei'rah, a wood or meadow, riverbank or stony mountain pasture that she had never seen before. Yet Ko was always there to meet her—and

Touriq with him, often—always repeating, "My beard knew, daughter. I had only to follow my beard." The satyr's presence remained all that she could ever take for granted: Woodmont passed straightforwardly through summer and into autumn as the days slipped by, but Joey could as easily step from southern California beach weather into cool, sudden rain as from the fire-haunted Santa Ana winds to the serene blue silence of a spring night in Shei'rah. There was no logic to it, no pattern that she could discover. Joey settled gladly for gratefulness and mystery.

She began to bring a drawing pad and a few pens with her each time she crossed the Border, having determined to map Shei'rah in as much detail as she could. Ko and Touriq guided her as she asked, forever patient and willing, if somewhat bemused; and the brook-*jalla*, who never left her stream, turned out to know the route and origin of every watercourse in the land, as intimately as though she had been born in each bed. "We just know," she said when Joey voiced her amazement. "Your people know those things you tell me about—what word is it?—*elections, rollerblades*? We *jallas* know water. Simple."

But Shei'rah resisted being known, resisted with an almost physical vigor. Hills seemed to shift their profiles even while Joey was shading them into her map; valleys and river gorges not only squirmed aside under her pen, but most often appeared unrecognizably different when she looked away and then tried to find them again. She never learned the contours of the land: there were no borders but the Border. Beyond that, she slowly began to understand, only the fleeting music of its unicorn lords gave true shape to Shei'rah, *and I'm the only one who can give the music a shape, so it'll be real in my world. So people will know.* That time she hurried home with the full moon, and uttered not one word of protest when John Papas told her

111

that she had botched the entire chord-voicing study he had written out for her. She sat down at his desk and redid the exercise promptly and perfectly. John Papas felt her forehead, only half-joking.

"Starting to look like something," he said one afternoon, playing over on an old clarinet what she had set down so far. "What kind form exactly, I couldn't tell you, but something for sure. Maybe we call it the Unicorn Sonata, what do you think?" Joey said it was all right with her.

Friends of John Papas's began to appear at the music shop: quiet men and women who said little, but who listened with such intensity as Joey played that she grew uncomfortable and taciturn herself, though their eyes were wide and their expressions dazedly rapturous. John Papas told her later that none of them had ever heard such music, and that they never had a notion of what to say to her afterward. "You make them *shy*, you understand that? These are people, listen, they play their Strads, their Kohnos, their Boesendorfers all over the world, for kings, queens, movie stars, and they're scared, they are *scared* to talk to Josephine Angelina Rivera, she goes to Ridgecrest Junior High. How about *that*, hah, kid? Now maybe you work a little harder on those inversions, right?" Mustache untrimmed, hair disheveled for days, he was a positive shambles of pride.

INDIGO APPEARED TWICE that summer. Each time he carried the silver-blue horn, and each time he leaned gracefully against the counter, lifted the horn to his lips and brought the nights and dawns of Shei'rah into the fusty little shop, playing the Eldest and the *criyaqui* alike, until even the corner cobwebs that Joey could never reach sparkled with moonlight, and Joey slammed the piano keys in frustration. Each time John Papas had somehow amassed more gold to offer him—not only coins, but jewelry and even metalwork—yet each time Indigo haughtily pronounced it too little, though Joey could feel his indecision as far down in herself as she felt the laughter of the brook-*jalla.*

Once, with John Papas momentarily out of earshot, she demanded, "You don't want to sell it, do you? You're just playing around, you *know* you'll want to go home someday. Why do you keep fooling around like that?"

Indigo answered her with something like wonder, "What do you care, Outworlder? Shei'rah is not your home, and its people are not yours, however much you pretend. Why should you care?"

"Because I've got a lot more friends there than I do here," Joey retorted. "Because I miss it more than I miss this place. That makes it my home, sort of."

Indigo grinned bitterly at her, shaking his beautiful head.

"Then this world of yours should be *my* home, but it is not, and it never will be. Shei'rah will still be my home when I have at last left it forever. And even so, I choose to be here. When I am suitably paid for what I am giving up."

THE SUNDAY NIGHT before school began was also the last night before the new moon. Joey briefly considered visiting Abuelita at another time, but established customs mattered a great deal to her grandmother in these days. "They are all I have left now, 'Fina," she had said once to Joey. "People my age, the *niños* are gone, the friends are gone, the body is going—what stays but the way you like to do things? If I didn't have my foolish old habits, I wouldn't remember who I was, do you know that?"

Joey worked out the day's timing very precisely. The moon

would rise in the late afternoon: if she caught the right buses she could still be home in plenty of time for dinner. In spite of the fact that her family would never miss her or know how far away from them she had been, she found herself, to her own surprise, clinging hard to them on those days when she planned to cross the Border.

She got everything ready in advance—by now she knew exactly what to stuff into her backpack for a visit to Shei'rah—and even remembered to bring a picture book to show to the brook-*jalla*, who could not conceive of such a thing. That done, she set out for Silver Pines, where Abuelita waited downstairs on the little bench.

"Your hair looks funny," Joey said. "What's all that white stuff in it? Your hair isn't white."

Abuelita laughed and slapped her sides until her brown skin turned almost pink. "I just stopped coloring it, 'Fina. I have been dyeing my hair for, oh, years, years. Because Ricardo liked it so much that way, all black. Now it is too much trouble, Ricardo will just have to take me as I am." She hugged Joey, then held her at arm's length, still laughing. "And you never knew, truly? I love you, 'Fina."

They had completed their first circuit of the little park when Abuelita used her free left hand to remove a gold bracelet, inset with ivory, from her right wrist and deftly fasten it on her granddaughter's arm before Joey knew what was happening. "Push it up a little, child. Your arm's too skinny."

Joey halted in her tracks. "You can't *do* that," she blurted, shocked back into English. "Take it back, Abuelita, it's too valuable. You can't just give something like that to a kid." She fumbled with the delicate old catch, trying to get the bracelet off.

Abuelita stopped her with a hand over hers. "'Fina, it was

always yours, since you were born. I want to see you wear it now, here, not looking down from heaven. That's too faraway, heaven, my eyes aren't so good anymore." When Joey's own eyes promptly filled with tears, the old woman scolded her. "Now don't you start carrying on like your brother. It's only a bracelet, it's only a grandmother, it's only life. No worse, no better, like I told you—only life, that's good enough for anybody."

"But I don't have anything to give *you*," Joey sniffed.

Abuelita gave her one of her gently scornful looks. "Even coming from a little girl, *that* was so silly we won't waste time talking about it. The worth is in the reason, not the gift. Anybody can give away a piece of jewelry, but nobody else could ever give me 'Fina. From the day you were born, what more could I ask?"

She paused abruptly, standing very still, a hand cupped behind one ear. "What is that? What am I hearing?"

Joey caught her breath, not daring to speak. Far and faint, but clear as her own heartbeat, the music sported up over the two freeways, mocking and loving, happily contradicting itself in every cadence: eternally, ridiculously alluring. And Abuelita heard it. Joey would have recognized the music of Shei'rah in her grandmother's face if she herself had gone stone deaf to it.

Abuelita unconsciously put her other hand to her breast, her eyes gone young with yearning. "That," she whispered. "The dream music. You could give me that."

"The dream music." Someone who was not Joey seemed to be speaking, a long way away. "You can hear it?"

"Every night," Abuelita said. "Every night, all night, I don't know how long. I dream such strange places, 'Fina, you wouldn't believe how strange. Faces, animals, such things—and always that music. Once I told Brittany—that's my nurse, the *names* they have—and she gave me a shot. So I don't tell anybody now, about the music. Just you."

Later, when there were all kinds of explanations immediately necessary, and not one forthcoming that would have been believed, Joey never once doubted what she had answered in that moment.

"Okay," she said. "Okay, Abuelita. Let's go back inside and get your coat, and maybe a couple of other things. I'll take you to the dream music."

In the end, they had to leave Silver Pines without permission. Abuelita was scheduled for massage therapy that afternoon, for one thing; for another, residents were never supposed to leave the grounds in the sole company of minors. Besides, *Harold and Maude* was being shown that evening, and the notion of an old woman being ready to miss *Harold and Maude* was vaguely suspicious on the face of it. They missed two buses before Abuelita finally took matters into her own hands and led Joey to the rear gate, whose attendant kept a forbidden Walkman in his uniform pocket and looked up for nothing less than a truck's airhorn. They slipped past without interrupting a single snap of his fingers.

As long as Joey could remember, Abuelita had always been the adventurer of her family, the adult most likely to suggest digging to China, exploring a deliciously frightening vacant shack, or rowing to Baja California across a summer lake. But that Abuelita, with whom Joey had so often trudged halfway across town in search of a favorite gypsy palm reader, a Maria Felix or Cantinflas movie, or a childhood friend from Las Perlas, had seemed very nearly as tireless as her granddaughter; and this Abuelita, so few years later, was already plainly weary after the long bus rides, though she neither complained nor asked for explanations. The music of Shei'rah still held all her deep attention, still flowered in her eyes; but she was limping within a few blocks' walk, and under the brown Indian skin Joey saw a frightening pallor spreading.

Another block. The moon's up already, good. One more block to Alomar, and then we'll be in Shei'rah and it'll be all right. She'll be all right once we cross into Shei'rah.

But the Border was gone.

Leaving Abuelita to rest against the corner mailbox, Joey cast frantically around in every direction, making increasingly forlorn dashes down an alley or halfway across a street—all in vain. The music could still be heard under the Valencia traffic; but there was no familiar dance in the darkening air, nor the least intimation of another world breathing in its own silver morning a single step away. The Border was gone.

Abuelita was waiting patiently at the mailbox. Joey turned and walked slowly back to her. She said, "Abuelita, I can't take you where the music's coming from. It's that place I told you about, and I knew how to get there, but I can't find it anymore. I'm sorry. I'm just so sorry."

Her grandmother smiled and stroked her hair. "Never mind, 'Fina. You can tell me about it on our way back, and that will be almost as good. It's all *right*, 'Fina, don't cry."

"It's not all right," Joey said. "I really, really wanted to take you to Shei'rah. Because it's special, it's too special to explain, and there's nobody else in the world I could ever show it to. And now it's gone, I've just lost it, and I'll never find it again, and you'll never *know*." No one but a grandmother could have made out the last words.

Abuelita held her, there on the street corner, crooning deeply to her. "'Little, little 'Fina, you still don't make a sound when you cry, do you, *mi corazón*? Never mind, then, never mind. Abuelita will believe anything you tell her, don't I always?" Joey felt her looking up suddenly, felt her entire body stiffen and straighten with anger. In English Abuelita said sharply, "Excuse me, we are private together here. Go away."

Indigo's voice answered her, sardonically formal. "I would be very pleased. But perhaps you should ask *her* first." Joey whirled in Abuelita's arms and saw him, coolly beautiful as ever in jeans, graffiti-splattered T-shirt, and the blue windbreaker. He was carrying the silver-blue horn. His eyes looked almost black under the twilight fragment of moon. He said quietly, "The Border has shifted. There will be a greater shifting soon, very soon, but you can still reach the Border. It is not far."

Joey stared at him. "You came to show us the way? Why? Why should you bother?"

For the first time, Indigo's smile was wry and quizzical enough almost to be human. "I don't know. I really do not know. Come."

Abuelita said to Joey in Spanish, "You know him? I wouldn't trust him for a minute. *Much* too pretty."

Joey laughed helplessly and hugged her. "Abuelita, this is Indigo. It's a long story. Indigo, this is Senora Alicia Ifigenia Sandoval y Rivera. This is my grandmother."

To her amazement, the boy took Abuelita's hand with immense courtesy, bowed over it and kissed it as though saluting a queen. Abuelita caught her breath, but then smiled and nodded: a queen receiving her accustomed due. Indigo said, "If you wish to see Shei'rah again, come now." Joey looked at Abuelita, who said, "I have to get back to the home, 'Fina. This Shei'rah, it won't take too long?"

"Not long at all," Joey answered her. "I absolutely promise, you'll be back at Silver Pines before they ever know you've been gone. I promise, Abuelita."

"Well," her grandmother said. "Okay, then. *Vamonos, chicos!*"

Abuelita stepped out bravely, following Indigo as he led them away from Alomar Street, heading, surprisingly, straight for the business district. But she was limping badly now, and it very quickly became impossible for Joey and her to keep up with Indigo's brisk, floating strides. When Joey finally called to him he turned, half a block ahead, and waited impatiently until they caught up. Joey said, "You're going to have to carry her. You're going to have to change."

Indigo laughed outright, the sound uncharacteristically harsh and direct. "I am not your little Touriq. I do not carry."

Abuelita was looking back and forth from one of them to the other. Joey said, as carefully as she had ever said anything, "Listen to me. This is my grandmother. I don't care if you live forever, you will never in your life meet anyone like her. She is going to see Shei'rah if it's the last thing I ever do, which I'm starting to think it probably will be. So you are going to carry her there—two legs or four, that's up to you. Just don't you mess with me, Indigo!"

She had not realized that she was shouting until she finished. Her throat hurt, and an astonished Eldest was gaping at her, and somewhere Abuelita was saying proudly in English, "That's my 'Fina. I don't know what she's talking about, but she is a *cookie!*" And across a parking lot, beyond the cold lighted window of a furniture store—*oh, not far, not far!*—the music of Shei'rah called to them.

Indigo looked at Joey without answering for what seemed a very long time. It was early yet, but the streets around them were already almost empty, except for commuters' cars heading home. A couple of boys on bicycles went by, followed by a cruising police car, whose driver gave Indigo, Abuelita, and Joey a mildly curious glance in passing. Joey heard a train whistle, and the iron coughing of store-window shutters coming down.

"There," Indigo said finally. "There you are. The Lord Sinti himself would never have spoken to me so. That took a mortal child with no manners, and no patience, and no understanding of anything important. And still you question why I would rather live on this side of the Border." He smiled then. "Very well. I will change, as you ask."

Joey turned quickly to Abuelita and gripped her shoulders gently. She said in Spanish, "Abuelita, listen, please. Whatever happens, whatever Indigo does, please don't be scared. It's just something he knows how to do, that's all, and he's just doing it to help us. Promise me you won't be scared."

Her grandmother looked up at her, eyes wise and tired under turtle lids. In English she replied, "I told you, I don't know what you're talking about. Let him do whatever he does and stop worrying for me. I'm too old to be much frightened anymore, 'Fina." She put Joey's hands down.

Indigo stepped back from them. He shook his head and shoulders violently and opened his mouth silently. Something invisible seemed to seize hold of him, to shake him between its jaws until he began to fray, began to lose all definition, flying out and apart in every direction. Abuelita gasped and caught hold of Joey's hand, but she made no other sound.

There on the street corner, in a Southern California suburb, with the San Diego Freeway mumbling in the distance, Indigo dissolved before their eyes and simultaneously flowed back together in his new form: cloven-hooved, daintily bearded, whiter in this world than in his own. Joey could see by a street light that his horn was not uniformly white, but a deeper shade at base and tip, like snow-shadows. He bowed his head before Abuelita, and she sighed like a lover.

"He's going to carry you on his back," Joey said. "It'll be okay, he'll be very careful." Indigo knelt down at the curb.

Abuelita looked long at him, then at Joey, and then at the dark sky. She said quietly, in a Spanish so formal that Joey hardly recognized it, "Ricardo, perhaps this is the way I am supposed to come to you. May it be so." Then, moving with the agility and confidence of a young girl, she swung herself up on Indigo's back. She took tight hold of his mane as he stepped slowly forward.

"What about me?" Joey protested. "I'm totally beat, I can't keep up with you. Can't I ride too?"

Indigo cocked a bright, amused eye at her. He quickened his pace deliberately, and Joey panted along beside him, grabbing Abuelita's ankle for support. "When the Border shifts again," he said, "it will not return to this place. You must be sure to leave Shei'rah in time."

"What time? What do you mean? How are we supposed to know?" Indigo ignored Joey's questions completely. He had veered away from the downtown streets now, and Joey realized with growing anxiety that he was heading directly toward the San Diego Freeway. She looked up at Abuelita, who was sitting erect on the white unicorn's back, her face young with wonder, lips moving wordlessly, her black-and-white hair surging loose around her head. *She's not scared, Grandpa. Oh, she's not scared at all.*

A car was honking again and again behind them. Joey had an instant to look back and glimpse a windshield crowded with open-mouthed young faces before Indigo caught the back of her shirt in his teeth and whisked her effortlessly off the ground and up before Abuelita, who steadied her as she scrabbled for balance. Then Indigo was pounding up the on-ramp and straight out into freeway traffic, and now the car horns were squalling madly, brakes yowling, and headlights careering in every direction like a startled school of fish as drivers tried to slow down, speed up, change lanes, and avoid colliding with the impossible all at once. Too numb to be frightened, Joey closed her eyes and clung to Indigo's mane, feeling Abuelita's calm hands on her waist, steadying her. Abuelita said in her ear, "It is all right, 'Fina. Nothing bad will happen to us." It sounded to Joey as though her grandmother were laughing.

Indigo swung left and left again, slipping between cars and vans and thunderblatting trucks as easily as the coolest California driver. A grassy island appeared on the left: he leaped smoothly to its skinny haven and stood still, ignoring the dark shapes streaking by on either side, and the occasional death-wail of a fender as cars driven by people looking backward shouldered into each other. Through the flashing bedlam, Indigo said clearly, "You would never have found it without me. Remember that."

He took two deliberate paces forward, to the far edge of the traffic island. Shei'rah's bright noon blossomed in silence around them. Behind Joey, Abuelita said softly, "Oh."

Chapter Nine

Joey had carefully prepared herself to calm Abuelita, to pet away an old woman's fear and bewilderment, but it did not happen so. Her grandmother's soft cry of wonder as she slipped gracefully from Indigo's back was for the meadow that had been Joey's earliest sight of Shei'rah. "*Ay*," she whispered, stooping to bathe both hands in the orange-tongued flowers, "*ay, que milagro*." When she looked up at Joey her face was a face Joey had never known, a child's birthday face. "*Ay*, 'Fina, you did it. You gave me the music."

Joey hugged her, at the same time casting a watchful glance at the brilliant sky. "We better move into the woods. The *perytons* come over here all the time." Indigo had disappeared without a word.

"*Perytons*." Abuelita tried it out, stroking Joey's hair. "*Peritonos*. They sound pretty." She looked over Joey's shoulder, and her caressing hand suddenly stopped moving. Joey turned quickly. The Lord Sinti was approaching them.

Joey could not remember seeing the black unicorn in full

day: she knew him as a creature of dusk and dawn, twilight and shadow, deeply present, but never fully visible. Now, pacing deliberately toward them, he seemed even darker for the sunlight, so black that everything but his blackness hurt Joey's eyes. He held his head high, so that the excrescences sealing his own eyes blazed turquoise in the sun, and the music of Shei'rah, sounding closer than Joey had ever heard it, sported around him like escorting dolphins. *Showing off for Abuelita,* she thought absurdly, feeling tears and giggles jostling in her throat.

Sinti moved past her with no sign of recognition and went straight to Abuelita, lowering the black horn until it brushed the hem of her dress. Abuelita reached out slowly, wonderingly, to touch the place where it sprang from his forehead. She said, "I dreamed this. I dreamed you."

"We dreamed each other," the Lord Sinti said. His voice was a stillness in Joey's racketing mind. "Welcome, Alicia Ifigenia Sandoval y Rivera."

"Alicia Ifigenia Josefina," Abuelita corrected him. She squeezed Joey's hand, but she went on staring at Sinti. The black unicorn said, "Once in a great while it happens that a dream in your world touches a dream in Shei'rah. It is a rare thing, but it does happen."

Joey noticed in a dazed, far-off sort of way that she was hearing Sinti in English, but that Abuelita was answering briskly in Spanish. "A rare thing, you say? You should come to the Silver Pines Guest and Rest Home. It's full of old ladies like me, all of us dreaming away about a place like this. What else is there for us, tell me that? If I dreamed you every night ever since I came there, night after night, who knows what those other *viejas* are dreaming?"

She stroked Sinti's neck, and Joey saw the eldest of the Eldest move against the touch like a housecat. He said, "But I dreamed you too, and I am not a grandmother in a Silver Pines." He turned his blind head toward Joey. "When she first came, I thought she was you. I thought I must have dreamed the wrong time."

Abuelita put her free arm around Joey's shoulders. "My 'Fina *is* me, only better. The new improved model." Her face turned somber as she put her hands gently over the black unicorn's eyes. "I didn't dream you blind, *pobrecito*. What is this?"

"It's happening to all of them," Joey told her. "The oldest first, then the . . . the little ones." She thought of Touriq, and wished him there.

Abuelita touched the black unicorn's eyes again. "This, I have to remember what we did in Las Perlas. We were too poor to have doctors, but there was something . . . I will remember."

Looking around them at the meadow, she sighed contentedly. "Well," she said. "Who will show me around this fine place?"

The brook-*jalla* was jealous of Abuelita for a little while. Having no family herself, except for the intense awareness of one another that all *jallas* have, however solitary, she immediately took Joey and Abuelita's intimacy as a rejection. Strangely, she understood this supplanting, or thought she did. To her, Abuelita's age was an astonishing miracle, her wrinkled brown skin and white hair gifts to be helplessly envied. "When you can be all the time with someone so beautiful," she said reasonably to Joey, "why would you ever bother with a common brook-*jalla*?" Not until Abuelita sat serenely down on the bank, dangling her arthritic feet in the water, and began to read aloud from the book Joey had brought in her backpack did the stream-sprite even draw near. Joey wisely went off with Touriq, and returned alone some hours later to find the two of them sound asleep. The brook-*jalla's* head was on Abuelita's lap, and she was clutching the picture book in both wet, webbed hands.

BEING IN SHEI'RAH WITH ABUELITA was, quite simply, the happiest time Joey had known in her life. It was also something more than she had bargained for: her grandmother, as spirited and curious as though seventy years had stepped aside, insisted on going everywhere, exploring everything, learning all. Joey said to Ko, "It's like babysitting a three-year-old. Turn around and she's trying to get a real close look at a *jakhao*, or else she's wandering out in the open picking flowers, happy as a clam, right exactly where the *perytons* could have picked *her*. Happy as a clam." She laughed and shrugged. "Yesterday I lost track of her for one single minute, and couldn't find her till after sundown. I was really scared. You know where she was? Go ahead, guess."

"Off with some of my younger cousins." Ko looked at the ground. "I am sorry, daughter."

"Oh, she had a ball, believe me," Joey said. "She just had a great time boogieing through the woods. I can't believe it. It's like finding a whole other grandmother, somebody I don't even know, hardly." She sighed. "I'm really going to hate having to take her home. When it's time."

But just when that time would be, neither Ko nor the Eldest could tell her. The most she learned, from Touriq's mother Fireez, was that a true Border Shift—as opposed to the casual wobble that had moved the Border merely to the middle of the San Diego Freeway—broke all the rules of passage between the two worlds. "There need not be a moon—a Shift can happen on any day or night at all. But the moment when we may cross over is very brief, much shorter than usual. And the crossing place changes, as you know." She admonished Touriq for playing too roughly with a baby satyr, and turned back to Joey. "I will tell you this. Watch the *shendi*."

"The *shendi*," Joey repeated. "The little dragons?"

Fireez nodded. "Where they are, the Border will be during this time. Watch them always. Tell your grandmother." The seafoam unicorn regarded her out of the serene, depthless eyes that always made Joey lightheaded to meet for long. "It will be farewell, Josephine."

Except for Sinti, the Eldest rarely used her name. Joey felt her throat tighten. "Maybe not. I mean, maybe the Border'll only move to San Francisco or someplace like that. Even Yuba City, that'd be something. I've got an uncle in Yuba City."

Touriq pressed close against Joey, shoving his head into her chest and stepping on her feet. Fireez said, "This Shift will take Shei'rah very faraway. I can feel it." She hesitated, brushing her horn quickly against Joey's cheek, and then added, "Those of us who live now in your world . . . I think they will never find the Border again, but perhaps you may. If you do, tell them. Watch for them and tell them where we are, Josephine."

"Yes," Joey whispered. "Yes, I will."

SHE CONTINUED TO DRAW her maps and pictures of Shei'rah, to sketch its life with a newly savage intensity. Thanks to her studies with John Papas, she was able now to scrawl on improvised staff paper fragments of the music that was as much a part of her daily breath here as the fragrance of flowers whose names she still did not know. The brook-*jalla* watched her in absolute fascination and uncharacteristic silence, finally asking, "What will you do with this, my sister? When you have Shei'rah's singing all snared fast between those black lines?"

"Well, I'll give it to people," Joey said awkwardly. "I mean, back where I come from there are all kinds of people who'd love to play the music of the Eldest. They can learn it from what I'm writing right now, and then they'll play it all over the world. My world, on the other side of the Border."

"Ah," said the brook-*jalla*. "And what then?"

"How would I know?" Joey demanded. "I mean, these are grown people, I'm just a kid, what do I know? They'll just play it, that's all, and maybe I'll be famous and be on television. And don't start, I already told you about television."

The brook-*jalla* stretched languidly in the water and snatched up a fish without apparently looking at it. Nibbling thoughtfully and precisely, as though eating corn on the cob—Joey always looked away—she remarked, "But you will not have me." Joey did not answer. The brook-*jalla* said quietly, "I understand about writing now, about books and pictures, even about television. But none of that is me. You may draw my picture, you may write down every word I say, but when all that is done, you will still not be swimming in my stream with me, still not hear me call you *sister*. So it is all silly. Come and catch fish."

Keeping track of the *shendi* was even harder than riding herd on Abuelita. *Shendi* mate for life, and most often live in clan-groups with other pairs; but none of the dragon clutches Joey knew could be found in any of the hot dry places where they normally laid their eggs and raised their palm-sized kits. Late one afternoon she finally came across a small covey in a shallow ravine of Sundown Wood, sheltering in a damp hollow log—a disturbingly unlikely choice for *shendi*. Abuelita was standing some distance off, watching the kits pretending to fly and the adults watching her. The Lord Sinti was with her.

Joey ran to Abuelita and hugged her hard. In her best Spanish

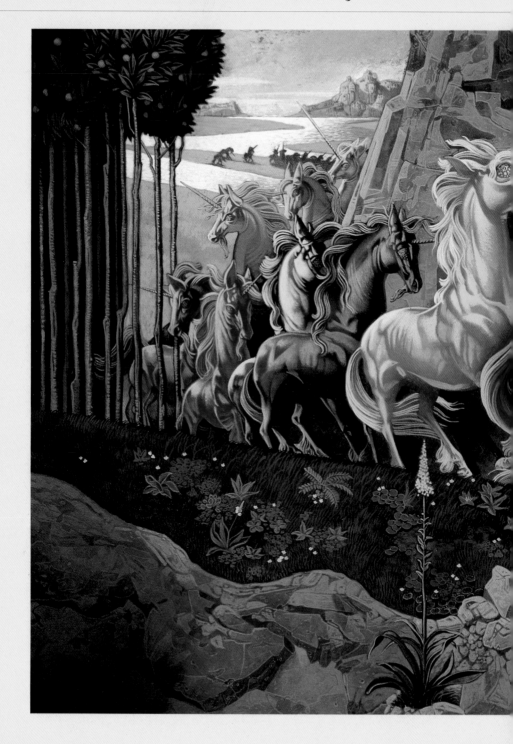

she said, "Grandmother, from now on you must stay very near me at all times. We may have to leave here in a great hurry."

Abuelita smiled. "The only nice thing about being as old as I am, 'Fina, is that you don't have to do anything in a hurry anymore." She winked and nodded toward the black unicorn. "*He* knows."

Sinti said to Joey, "You were wise to seek out this place. I think this is where the one crossing point will be, when the Shift comes."

"You think," Joey said. "You're not sure." Sinti did not reply. Joey took a deep breath and said, "Indigo says that the Eldest can survive across the Border. It's true, I've seen them." The black unicorn waited, unmoving. "And—and he says that the Eldest don't live forever. He says that's a lie. . . ." Her voice trailed off with the last words.

"Child, no one lives forever," Abuelita said. "That is not allowed. I could have told you that." Sinti seemed to draw in on himself, becoming at once bigger and darker, and somehow less solid: a great twilight shadow, weighed down by his own shadowy wisdom.

"Perhaps that is what binds us together," he said, "your people and mine, your world and ours. Our lives are so much longer than yours, far longer even than the lives of the *tirujai*, so long that we truly forget at times that we are not immortal. And yet we fear death just as deeply as you do—more, surely, because Shei'rah is so much kinder to us than I think your world is to you. It shames us, this knowledge that we die, and if we keep it from our young ones we keep it from ourselves too, as best we can. I do believe we were different once, but that was before even my time, and this is the truth now."

"*Ay*, you should definitely come to the Silver Pines Guest

and Rest Home," Abuelita said gently. "If you want to see what comes of lying to your children."

Sinti was still facing Joey. "I told you once: from the beginning, in every one of your generations, there have always been Eldest who crossed the Border in human shape. What I did not say was that some never returned, but vanished forever among you. Such was their choice, and we honor it, but we do not encourage it." He turned away abruptly, but his voice continued to resound ruefully in Joey's mind. "Perhaps our blindness is the result of what we have refused to see. It may be so."

Watching him pass into the blue trees, Abuelita said to Joey, "He talks so beautifully. Your grandfather used to talk like that after the second glass of *pulque.*" The long, loose dress Joey had persuaded her to bring when they set off together was ragged at the hem and stained by the earth and grasses of Shei'rah; but there was a warm color in her brown cheeks that Joey had never before seen there, and her eyes were sparkling like the brook-*jalla's* stream in the afternoon sun. She said, "Thank you for bringing me here, 'Fina. Wherever it is."

"I don't know," Joey said. "I mean, it's okay for me, but when you get down to it, there's not really a whole lot to do in Shei'rah, you know? It probably gets pretty boring and all for you."

Abuelita smiled. "'Fina, back at Silver Pines they have all kinds of things for old people to do. There is golf, there is Ping-Pong, writing classes, costume parties, putting on plays. . . . You can even learn to do karate and give massages if you want. But this is the first time in a very long while that I am just able to *be.* Sit and think about nothing all day. Smell flowers I never smelled in all my life. Tell stories to that little girl in the water, or go drinking and dancing with the hairy people, those funny-smelling ones. Nothing to explain to anyone. When you are old like me, 'Fina, you will understand what a good thing it is to have nothing to explain."

One of the *shendi* kits, eluding its parents' watchfulness for a moment, slither-stalked up to Abuelita, propped its scaly, clawed front feet on her shoe and hissed at her. Abuelita dropped comfortably down onto her heels, holding out her hand, cooing, "*Ven aqui,* little treasure, little wickedness, *ven aqui.*" The dragonlet scurried backwards, fell over itself, picked itself up, and warily approached the alluring brown fingers once again. Abuelita looked past it at the male and female, now raising their black-ribbed turquoise wings and arching their necks in warning, and said clearly, "I am no one. I am a tree, a stone, a bit of sunlight, no more." Very slowly, the wings came down.

Joey said, "I can't stand it. I've been trying to get close to them for *months*!" The *shendi* kit made up its mind at last and scrambled into Abuelita's cupped hand. Without rising she brought it close to her face, and the two of them gazed long at each other.

"Well, there is another thing about being old," Abuelita said. "People aren't so frightened of you." She put the kit down on the ground and it strutted back to its parents, looking twice its original size. The female promptly knocked it flat, and then gathered it in to her. Abuelita said, "'Fina, I *know* we can do something about this blind business. I'll remember any minute now."

"Abuelita, did you hear what I was telling you?" Joey asked. "We might have to get going really, really suddenly, or we'll cross back over and come out in China or somewhere."

"Mmm," Abuelita murmured. She was still squatting on her heels, closing her eyes. "Wouldn't that be something, China, after all?" Joey gave up then, and flopped down beside her, lying on her stomach and watching the little dragons.

Chapter Ten

When Abuelita did remember, it happened in the dead of a moonless night so warm that she and Joey were sleeping in the open, curled comfortably together on a sheltered hillside not far from Sundown Wood. She sat up as though she had never been asleep, slapped Joey's hip and announced loudly, "*Oro! Oro* it is!"

"A little louder," Joey mumbled, too groggy to speak Spanish. "Might be a *peryton* out there somewhere who didn't hear you." Abuelita was already on her feet, clapping her hands and turning in small, rapturous circles. "Gold, 'Fina! For the eyes, gold, *yes*! The way we did in Las Perlas!"

Joey sat up slowly, shaking her head on her stiff neck. "Abuelita, you didn't have any gold in Las Perlas. You didn't even have running water."

"Running water, no. Money, no, of course not. But *gold*!" Her grandmother squatted down beside Joey, talking earnestly but laughing through the words. "Always there was some gold somewhere, especially in a little poor town like Las Perlas. A bracelet,

133

like that one I gave you, earrings, a watch, an old medal maybe, even a shoe buckle. You'd be amazed what's gold, and who might have a small bit of it. Just in case, *tu sabes*?"

"Like Mr. Papas." Joey knuckled her eyes, trying to get them unstuck. "Mr. Papas, hanging onto all those coins in a little box, just in case. And his friends, the same way." Her yawn muffled the last words. "Okay, so what about the gold? What about the eyes?"

"*Pues*, the one thing we had plenty of down in Las Perlas was blind people, people with bad eye trouble. Children especially." Elbows resting on her knees, Abuelita leaned forward, clasping her hands in front of her. "So. Someone would turn up a ring, a bangle, and you would melt it down and add a few things to it. Pound it in a *metate*, make a—what? an *embrocacion*?—make a sort of an ointment and rub it right on the eyes. It was hot, I remember that. I don't know if that was the gold, but I remember how it felt in my hand." She sighed vastly and tenderly. "*Ay*, you missed some things, 'Fina, not growing up in Las Perlas."

"I bet I did," Joey said. She was wide awake now, carefully reminding herself that Abuelita told many stories about Las Perlas. "So did it work? Did anybody ever get their sight back?"

"*La verdad*! People who could not see at all, in a little while they would begin to see again. This is the truth, 'Fina!"

Even without the moon, Abuelita's own eyes were brilliant with delight.

"Well, there aren't any gold watches in Shei'rah, I know that much—" Joey broke off, stood up quite slowly, and then asked, so softly that Abuelita had to strain to hear her, "What other stuff? What else did you put in?"

"Ah, now I have to think about *that*." Abuelita sighed and frowned and scratched her head. "What could it have been? What did we have? Leaves, there was one special leaf you had to grind up. You go find us some gold while I am remembering, 'Fina. These things come back slowly to an old woman. Go, go, I'll be here." Abuelita settled down on her haunches, tenting her fingers together, smiling off at nothing, looking as peaceful and permanent as a tree. And Joey, half-laughing, half-exasperated, and totally flummoxed, stumbled off through the darkness in search of gold.

In Joey's experience with the Eldest, there was never any point in looking directly for one or another of them. They came and found you, or they didn't. With this in mind, she skirted Sundown Wood until she came to the edge of the plain where she had first seen the young unicorns grazing and racing. Then she stood with her legs planted and her hands behind her back, and she spoke to Indigo in her mind. *Look, you don't like me, I don't know if you like anybody, except you were really nice to Abuelita. Well, this is about Abuelita, and it's about the Eldest going blind, so if that means anything to you I'm right here and we can talk. Okay? Okay, I guess that's it.* And then, because she was still feeling more than a little ridiculous, and giddy to boot, she added *This is Radio Free Woodmont, signing off,* and sat down to wait.

The sun was high, and the music of Shei'rah, which most often tended to swell with the dawn and gradually fade through the morning, had dwindled to a sweet whisper by the time Joey saw him. He came in human form, to her great surprise, and she got up and went to meet the small figure trudging across the plain.

There were few of the Eldest playing between them, and those paid no attention at all as Joey and Indigo faced each other. She thought he looked tired, and almost not beautiful.

"Thanks for coming," she said. Indigo favored her with a

long, cool stare, and Joey saw the blue-green smudging at the corner of his eyes for the first time.

"Yes," he said, answering her look. "Yes, and what of it? What have you to say to me?"

Joey spoke very fast, to keep herself from thinking. "We need gold. Me and Abuelita." Indigo's expression did not change in the slightest, but he blinked, which Joey took as a private triumph. "It's to fix your eyes, all of you, we'll melt the gold down and make some kind of ointment. Abuelita knows how to do it. Only we have to hurry, because the Border's going to shift any minute."

She waited for his gust of mocking laughter, as she had waited all morning, knowing that what came after that was what mattered. But he surprised her again by saying only, after a silence, "I have no gold. Ask your Papas Music if you want gold."

"He wouldn't give it to me," Joey said. "But he'd give you every scrap of gold he has. And he's got a whole lot more than he had the first time you came in. I think he's been calling all his friends and everybody."

"I see. So now I am to sell him my horn and give you the gold." Indigo's curious placidity was more alarming to Joey than his scorn would have been. A pair of very young unicorns danced past on their hind legs, fencing dramatically with their stubby horns and snorting like steam engines. The light breeze shifted suddenly, bringing the perfumed-ashes scent of yellow *shaya* flowers out of deepest Sundown Wood. Joey said, "Yes. Yes, that's it. That's what I'm asking."

Indigo shook his head in what might have been mockery, wonder, or both. "Let me be very sure of what you ask. You will have me go naked, without either horn or gold, into your world, where gold is everything, where if I have no money I am nothing, nothing, it does not matter that I am of Shei'rah, of the Eldest. "And if I do this, your grandmother will brew a magic potion that will help my people to see again. Have I understood you?" Joey realized then that he was trembling visibly; his voice cracked and split on the last words.

"I told you, yes," she repeated doggedly. "And when you're across the Border, in my world, I promise I'll do everything I know to help you. Mr. Papas will too. You'll have friends, you won't be like those others, the ones on the street and everything. I absolutely promise." After a moment she added, "There'd probably be some gold left over, anyway. Abuelita says it doesn't take that much."

Indigo smiled at her: not the slanted, sardonic smile she knew so well, but one that seemed to come slowly from very faraway, and not really to be meant for her. "No," he said. "I will not be like the others who have left Shei'rah, for I will not even have a horn to play on the street corners. I must depend on my wits and my friends, as you say, and perhaps that will be enough to make a life, and perhaps not. And I will never be able to return."

Joey tried to speak, but her mouth was too dry. Indigo asked very quietly, "Why should I do this?"

She never knew how long she looked back at him, with her head utterly empty of any thoughts at all. It seemed a very great, echoing while before she was even able to find words to think, *Abuelita, this is it. I have to say something really smart and meaningful right now, and you know I'm just your weird granddaughter. If I'm supposed to help the Eldest, you better help me fast, or we can just hang it up and go be roommates at Silver Pines.* She cleared her throat, fighting back the urge to yawn that always came on her when she was afraid.

"Because it's what you want," she said. "Because you know my world a lot better than I'll ever know yours, and you know what it's like, and you still want to live there just *because* it's like that. I mean, you're scared of it, that's why you keep almost selling Mr. Papas your horn and then not. And you ought to be scared, because it's a really, really scary world where I live. But that's why you want to be there, because it's not Shei'rah. And I don't think the gold ever mattered to you, not really. The gold's just an excuse for not *moving*. I do that all the time."

But her voice sounded parched and feeble as a winter grasshopper in her own ears, and her reasoning as pitiful as one of her brother Scott's lies earnestly explaining why he hadn't taken out the garbage. She felt herself running down, dwindling, dribbling away into silence before Indigo's strangely patient gaze. Abruptly she said, "No. No, forget it, don't listen to me, don't listen, I'm sorry, it's all wrong. I'm *sorry*."

She was already walking away by the time all the words were out, but Indigo's hand on her shoulder stopped her. "Wait," he said. "What is this? After all this talk, all this fuss, why now should I suddenly not listen to you?" He did not raise his voice, but the grip of his hand made Joey remember the hands of the *criyaqui* dragging her up into their tree.

She turned to face him. The dark blue eyes were once again as arrogantly questioning as the first day she had seen them, and the sideways set of his head as provoking. But she had his deep attention, as she thought she never had before. She shrugged and answered, "You're right, that's all. *I* wouldn't make the deal even for a ton of money, why am I asking you? Forget it, like I said, okay? My Abuelita's smart, she'll come up with something else. Don't worry about it."

Again she turned away, and again Indigo spun her back

toward him. Keeping his voice coldly conversational, he said, "I could cross the Border this moment, naked and empty-handed, and make my own way in your Woodmont, or anywhere else. Without any stupid help from you or your Papas Music. You know that."

"God, I forgot how contrary you are," Joey said wearily. "Now you'll do it just because I told you not to. You know what, Indigo? I'll tell you what. The hell with you. You do what you want, I have to get back to Abuelita. Send me a postcard, okay?"

She was already well into Sundown Wood, still framing her apology to Abuelita—*I blew it, I just blew the whole thing, it's my fault, he makes me so mad*—when Indigo finally caught up with her. Joey halted and waited silently while he stared at her as though he had never seen her before. She glowered back, realizing in some faraway place that she had not been afraid of him for a long time, and feeling something almost like regret.

Indigo sighed. "All the little music shops," he said. "All the music shops in all your splendid, horrible world, and I walk into the one that has Josephine Rivera in it. Oh, you should have been born in Shei'rah, Josephine Rivera. It would have spared both of us so much bother."

JOHN PAPAS ACCEPTED the horn almost reluctantly, asking Indigo, "You sure? Look—" with a nod at Joey—"*she* tells me about this thing, what it means, so I know what's what a little. You sure you want?"

"Oh, I always wanted," Indigo replied softly. "*Sure*—no, perhaps never—but I must act as if I were sure. Isn't that the first lesson of living in this world?" He pushed the silver-blue horn into John Papas's hands. "But it will cost you a great deal, as I told you it would."

John Papas lifted the horn slowly, as though it were far heavier than Joey knew it to be. "Not like it costs you. I know this too." He looked back and forth from Indigo to Joey, then sighed and nodded again. "Okay. Okay. I find you a box, you'll need."

They had to wait for the moon, the two of them sitting side by side at an outdoor coffee shop near the freeway. Indigo kept ordering *café mochas*—"My greatest discovery in your world so far! Who knows what other wonders lie ahead?"—and Joey kept trying to think of more things to warn him about, like muggers, cholesterol, tetanus shots, the Immigration and Naturalization Service ("*La migra*, Abuelita calls them—Indigo, remember, you have absolutely *got* to get a green card, some way!"), and the thinning ozone layer. Finally, just after she had explained what drive-by shootings were, he said with his old irritability, "Tell me something good about your world, something you like, something we do not have in Shei'rah. I can find the rest out for myself."

Joey thought for a long time before she answered him. "Well, cats are good. We can't have one, because I'm allergic, but cats are really nice." She felt as though all Shei'rah were watching her through Indigo's eyes, hungering for her true answer. "That man," she said. "Under the freeway. The one who was taking care of your friend? Who brought her pizza?" Indigo nodded. Joey said, "You were right, that's as good as we get. That's the best we have."

The Woodmont sky was so heavy and stagnant with smog that she could not tell when the moon had actually risen, but Indigo knew. He finished one more *café mocha*, wiped his mouth, grinned like a gleeful truant, and held out his hand. Joey sat still, unable to make herself rise from the table. Indigo said, "Come. I will walk you home."

She left him on the freeway island, her arms full of gold coins and jewelry and little religious statues, her eyes so bewildered with tears that Indigo had to turn her brusquely around, point her toward the Border, and tell her, "Go. Save my people's sight, or leave them with sticky, useless ointment filling their eyes. It does not matter. We do what we must."

"Mr. Papas will help you," Joey blubbered. "And I'll be back, and I'll help. It'll be all *right.*"

"It is all right now," Indigo said softly. "Why do you suppose the Eldest became blind in the first place?"

"What?" Joey tried to turn in his grasp. "What did you say?"

"Ask your grandmother." For just a moment Indigo's hands were friendly on her shoulders. "She will know, your Abuelita. Stop wriggling, 'Fina Rivera, mind that truck . . . *go!*" His hands went to the small of her back and he shoved her violently across the Border, and into the wild serenity of Shei'rah.

OBTAINING THE GOLD for Abuelita's eye salve turned out to be far easier than finding the exact herbs to go with it. Of the ones Abuelita remembered, some had no exact equivalent in Shei'rah, and had to be guessed at, no help for it; others were both known and dishearteningly rare. But they had the priceless help of the *tirujai,* who went everywhere and knew everything concerning plants; and the brook-*jallas* of the land proved prodigiously knowledgeable about anything that grew along running water. Joey's adopted sister even sought out Indigo's river-*jalla* acquaintance for advice; though how she persuaded her to supply the essential medium for the ointment—animal fat—and where she got it, Joey did not ask and never wanted to know. Abuelita was as matter-of-fact about this as about anything else, saying only, "How do you think we made this in Las

141

Perlas? Don't be such a squeamish, 'Fina." She was stirring up the mixture with her bare brown hands at the time.

Abuelita also eventually solved the problem of making a fire hot enough to melt gold. She accomplished this by persuading a number of adult *shendi* to concentrate their tiny but white-hot flames on a hollow that she had made in the damp sand of a riverbank and filled with Indigo's coins. When Joey demanded to know how she had communicated with the little dragons, her grandmother replied, "*Querida*, I make the night nurses at Silver Pines understand me. I can even talk to your father and mother, most times. Tell me, what's a bunch of little dragons to that?"

Ko had slipped off to the high desert and returned with a scarlet gourd almost as big as himself. Joey had never seen such a thing in that region, but Ko said they grew there in plenty if you knew where to look. It took an entire day to gouge through the gristly shell and hollow the gourd out; but when that was done Abuelita had a perfect cauldron in which to blend gold, tallow, crumbled leaves, bits of grass, and assorted extracts of sap and tree bark to her heart's content. She did this in complete privacy, not allowing even Joey near, whistling an ancient muleteers' song through her teeth. Then she spat into the gourd twice, said two or three words which were not Spanish at all, and called Joey to her. "So," she said. "Now we find out if we knew anything in Las Perlas or not. Maybe yes, maybe no."

Joey goggled at her in sudden alarm. "Maybe *no*? You said the stuff always worked."

"I said always?" Abuelita pulled on her lower lip and shrugged slightly. "Well, I'm an old woman, I forget some things. A little nothing town full of poor farmers, we used to try all kinds of crazy medicines. Anyway, that was Las Perlas. This is not Las Perlas."

"Indigo told me it wouldn't work," Joey said in a small voice. "But he sold his horn anyway."

Abuelita turned quickly, hugging and shaking and scolding her all at once. "'Fina, don't *worry* so about everything! We do the best we can, nobody asks of you more than that. If it works, if it doesn't work, Indigo knows we did our best. God knows too. Come on, you go get everybody here, it's time."

For all of Joey's constant fear of the Border shifting and stranding Abuelita and herself thousands of miles from home, her first sight of the Eldest of Shei'rah coming to be healed swept everything else from her mind. Abuelita had set up her gourd-cauldron over a small fire on the edge of a prairielike grassland bordered by the far desert hills in two directions, in a third by what the satyrs called the Summer Marshes, where many of them congregated during the warmest days. Thus Joey had a view of three long processions of unicorns stretching away as far as she could see, until their figures were lost in mist or sun-shimmer. Even on the plain she had never seen so many Eldest at once: she tried to count them, but lost track almost immediately. They were of every color, from *karkadann* red to a gold brighter than Indigo's coins, to the near-midnight blue of some of the *ki-lins*; the stately Eldest stood placidly while colts younger than Touriq racketed and curvetted around them; and the music of Shei'rah, clearer than Joey had ever heard it, mirrored and celebrated their variety, welling up on all sides as though neither earth nor air could contain it any longer. *Like people lining up for their flu shots*, she thought, and giggled absurdly, and then she turned aside and wept.

Abuelita squatted cross-legged behind her cauldron, anointing the caked, swollen eyes of each Eldest in turn—those like Touriq, who could still see, as well as the long-blind—greeting those she knew by name (and Joey was dumbfounded at how many there were, in how short a time), and repeating over and over, "Wait for a few days—three, four, whatever. If nothing changes, come back and we'll try again." She sat so all that day, dozed a few hours while the Eldest waited silently, and was back at it before the moon was down. When Joey offered for the twentieth or thirtieth time to take over, Abuelita replied, as always, "No, *gracias*, 'Fina. Better if it's me, I don't know why. I'm fine, don't worry. Yaradai, don't shake your head like that, I know it burns a little bit, leave it alone."

The whole process took two days and a night. The Lord Sinti came last, and when he bent his high black head into Abuelita's smeared, weary hands, she fell asleep but went on smoothing the salve into his eyes anyway. She slept more or less continuously for two days after that, so she missed the very first of the Eldest who returned to thank her. Their vision was hazed still, and untrustworthy, still flickering on and off, but it was true vision, not the shadow-sight that had had to serve them for so long, and even the grandest among them were gazing at the world around them and themselves in it with the eyes of wobbly legged colts. Like Joey on her first morning in Shei'rah, Abuelita woke surrounded by unicorns; and though they looked at her without speaking, she sat up instantly and said, "It worked, huh? *There's* one for Las Perlas!" She promptly fell asleep again, but the Eldest waited patiently, never stirring, until she woke a second time.

Chapter Eleven

It was Ko, as she might have expected, who came for them on the night when the Border shifted at last. Joey was awakened by his smell, rank and reassuring as ever, and sat up fast, turning to rouse Abuelita from her leafy bed. But Abuelita was already on her feet, peering through the darkness toward the log where the *shendi* had been when they lay down to sleep. The air felt hot and crackling against Joey's skin; there was a bitter, stormy taste to it. Ko said, "It is time to go, daughter. My beard knows."

Joey put her arms around him. She said, "I'm never going to see you again. Never."

"I stopped saying *never* on my hundredth birthday," the satyr answered. "Shei'rah will not disappear, nor will the moon, nor will the Border ever be closed to you or your grandmother. You will find it again, somewhere in your world—sooner than you think, perhaps. We shall be waiting." He held Joey gently and close against his malodorous chest.

Abuelita said, "'Fina, they're gone. The dragon things."

Joey and Ko whirled together and ran to the log. There was no sign of any of the *shendi*; even their odd coppery smell seemed to have dissipated. Panic took Joey by the throat then. "The Border! I don't know where the Border is! Ko, what'll I do, what do I do now?" The half-moon was barely in sight behind the trees.

"Calm," Ko said, turning helplessly this way and that. "Daughter, be calm." Abuelita sat down under a tree and began unhurriedly combing her hair.

Joey gripped Ko's shoulders and shook him hard in her terror. "Ko, we're going to be trapped on the other side of the world! How will I ever get Abuelita home? Ko, *please*, I have to get her home!"

Abuelita said quietly, "No, you don't, 'Fina." Joey and the satyr turned to stare at her, smiling in the dark under the tree. She said, "'Fina, I decided. I'm not going back."

Joey said, "*What?*" Ko's slit yellow eyes actually rounded in astonishment. Joey whispered, "Abuelita, what are you talking about? We have to go home."

"You have to, yes," her grandmother agreed placidly. "You have your family, your school starting, your whole life, everything waiting back there for you. And Indigo, you must find Indigo. But there is nothing waiting for me except Silver Pines and death. No, I like it much better here."

As Joey gaped at her, an ominous crash in the brush was immediately followed by Touriq's triumphant cry, "Oh, *there* you are!" The unicorn colt cantered into the ravine and went straight to Joey, bumping her with his horn as he nuzzled hard into his favorite place under her arm. "Why are you here?" he demanded. "The *shendi* are all sleeping up by the Three-Moon Pool, where the *karkadanns* bathe. What are you doing away down here?"

The next moments were always somewhat blurred in Joey's

memory. She recalled scrabbling in the leaves for her backpack and Abuelita's few belongings, and Ko furiously berating his beard for missing the flight of the *shendi*. "I should have *known* they might move at night! The nearer a Shift, the more restless and changeable they become." Then, with no transition at all, she and Abuelita were both on Touriq's back, plunging uphill through thorny, raking shrubbery, with Ko racing beside them, taking great bounds on his goat legs. Joey shouted a lot at Abuelita during that time, but her grandmother merely shrugged and pointed to her ears, smiling sweetly.

Joey had never seen Three-Moon Pool except from a distance, because of her lingering unease around *karkadanns*. The stone-set pond in the hills seemed too small for such great creatures, but there were always three or four at least splashing and bellowing in its green shade. On this night, however, it was empty, pale in the last angled rays of the vanishing moon. The *shendi* were nowhere to be seen.

"They are here, daughter," Ko said. "My beard will not betray us again." Joey slid off Touriq and helped her grandmother down. They stood holding each other's hands. Joey said, "Abuelita, this is crazy. What am I going to tell my folks, for God's sake?"

Abuelita fluttered one hand airily. "Tell them that I went back to Las Perlas. I have been threatening to do that for years." Her smile was suddenly not old and benign at all, but so youthfully mischievous that Joey's heart tried to soar out of her chest toward her. In English Abuelita said, "And do you know what, 'Fina? It is almost true."

"There's the Border," Touriq announced. "I *told* you!"

Halfway across the Three-Moon Pool, a curtain of pulsating color had trembled into being, turning the water to a jeweled tumult of moons. Joey tried not to look at it. She held Abuelita desperately, saying, "I don't want to leave you here. I'll miss you. Won't you miss me? Me and—and everybody?"

"I will miss you, my 'Fina," Abuelita said. "The way I miss your grandfather, I will miss you. Except that you will come back to see me here, somehow, just like every Sunday at Silver Pines, and he never can. The rest . . ." she held out one hand, palm down, and wobbled it dubiously in the air. "The rest, not so much." She hugged Joey once, quickly, and then stepped back, pointing toward the Border. "Go, go, *you* will miss your bus. Oh," and she suddenly gripped Joey's wrists tightly, "tell Indigo . . . well, just give him my love."

"Indigo!" Joey reached toward Abuelita again. "Indigo said to ask you why the Eldest were blind, only I forgot. He said you'd know."

"*Ay*, that boy." Abuelita shook her head, laughing a little. "It was that he has been trying so long to sell the horn for money. They can't do that, that's not what they are, what this place is. Things just start getting disordered, pulling apart, *comprendes*, 'Fina?"

"But he did sell it," Joey cried. "He's the only one, the only Eldest who ever sold his horn—"

"But not for *himself*." In the light of the Border, her grandmother's face seemed to pulse with meaning. "It is as I told you, the worth is in the reason. Go now, hurry. I love you, 'Fina."

The Border danced and reeled over the Three-Moon Pool. Joey looked at the water and then at Touriq, who said proudly, "On my back." Ko was silently there to help her mount. Joey leaned down to embrace him, herself unable to speak. The satyr whispered, "I was right to call you *daughter*, was I not?" Joey could only nod.

Touriq waded out into the pool, stepping high as a show horse on parade until the water was up to his hocks and Joey's shoes. She leaned over his neck as they approached the Border, telling him over and over, "This isn't goodbye, it isn't, I promise, Touriq. I'll find you again, it doesn't matter where the damn Border moves, I'll find Shei'rah again. I will."

"Oh, I know *that*," the unicorn colt answered her jauntily. "I'd never be here if I thought you were really leaving us." His horn rippled scarlet and green and violet in the glow of the Border.

The sky was raddled with light now, the darkness silvering in places to show the impatient dawn beneath. It seemed to Joey that she saw scores of half-hidden Eldest watching her—*seeing me*—from the trees beyond the Three-Moon Pool, whichever way she turned her head. The shadow of the Princess Lisha dipped her horn in salute, as did her great red companion; the Lady Fireez's voice floated softly through her mind, murmuring, "I will care for your grandmother as you have cared for my son. Go safely, mortal child."

She could not see the black Lord Sinti at all, but she felt his voice more clearly than any other. "Tell Indigo that we understand what he has done. If his great hunger to belong fully to your world brought on our blindness, his sacrifice has set us free, and perhaps himself as well. We will remember. Tell him this, Josephine Angelina Rivera."

By the time they reached the Border, Touriq was all but swimming, and Joey on his back was soaked above her waist, shivering in the dawn chill. The Border loomed above them, far grander and wilder than the softly shivering luminousness that Joey had come to take almost for granted. It made a huge, hollow sound like hot grease on a griddle.

"Well," Joey said. She stroked Touriq's neck, grimly bracing herself to slide into the water and flounder the last few yards. But the unicorn colt turned his head sharply, halting her with his horn. Simultaneously Sinti spoke in her one last time. "Do not try to swim—your clothes would pull you down. Stand up on Touriq's back and leap through the Border. Do as I tell you."

Joey hesitated, then kicked off her shoes and clambered very cautiously upright, waving her arms for balance. Touriq said suddenly, "Maybe I will come to you in your world when I am grown. One day you might just look up and there I'll be."

"No!" Joey said. The force of her response almost made her fall off his back. "No, Touriq, don't you *dare*! You stay where you are, promise me that! You promise me that right now."

Touriq mumbled something that might or might not have been an agreement. "Go on, then. Dig your toes in and jump, as hard as you can. I'll help you." He lowered his head slowly. "We must count together. . . . *one, two* . . ."

On *three* his back surged like a wave under Joey's feet, and she crouched and flung herself forward, straight into the flaring, hissing maelstrom of color—and as she did so, she felt the Shift begin. The Border turned instantly to smoke, gray swirling within slow gray, and Joey tumbled through it, tossed this way and that as randomly as a child's bath toy, losing all sense of time, all sense even of whether she was falling or rising through the endless smoke. She reached out, found her legs and drew them in close, wrapping her arms tight around them to make herself into a little ball, able to think only one coherent thought: *what happens if I come out back on the freeway?* She shut her eyes, desperately remembering Ko's dear stink. . . .

. . . and found herself bouncing and rolling between the rusty pumps of an abandoned gas station. The entire area for blocks around was fenced off for razing and new construction; Joey saw heavy machines parked everywhere, but no people at all. The afternoon sun was low, and there was a distant cold fragrance in the air, bringing such loneliness down on Joey so hard that she sat on the self-service island and wept with her head on her soggy knees. In time she stood up and tried to wring some of the water of the Three-Moon Pool out of her jeans, looking around slowly to get her bearings.

Okay. Okay. If it works like always, I've been to see Abuelita at Silver Pines, and I'm on my way home right now. Okay. I'll go home.

But she stood where she was for a while longer, gazing vaguely at the empty, half-erased streets without seeing them. There was not the slightest hint of the Border, nor could she hear a single impertinent note of the music of Shei'rah, no matter how intensely she listened for it. *But maybe I was never really hearing it at all. Maybe I just felt it inside, like the voices of the Eldest. I'll never know now.* She turned abruptly and walked away.

BUT SHE DID NOT GO home immediately. Evening found her in Papas Music, sitting at John Papas's desk and wearing his friend Mr. Provotakis's old bathrobe, while her jeans steamed in front of a small heater. John Papas was alternately asking questions, pouring more Greek coffee for her, and reminding her to telephone her parents, which she had already done. "The home's already called about Abuelita. I told them she was talking a lot about Las Perlas, so maybe she just finally took off. She'd have done that, Abuelita." Her voice trembled a little, and she covered it with a gulp of the coffee.

"You think they bought it?" John Papas asked. Joey shrugged wearily. "If they didn't, they will. Costs a lot of money to keep somebody in a home, they used to talk about it at night. They won't do a whole lot of looking, I don't think."

The two of them were both quiet for a time. John Papas said finally, "Melted them all down, huh? And he let her do it? Some kid, that Indigo." He nodded toward the silver-blue horn nestled in an old trombone case. "Now I feel funny, like maybe I ought to give this back to him. You think?"

"He wouldn't take it," Joey said.

John Papas nodded. "Well, I figure some way to make it up to him, best I can. You try to be fair. He still around, then?"

"He had to stay behind when Shei'rah . . . when Shei'rah moved." *Have to get used to saying it, thinking it, you have to, that's all. Indigo has to.*

"Some kid," John Papas repeated. He gestured toward the horn again. "Play now. Play that Shei'rah for an old man won't ever see it. Play, please."

Joey shook her head. "I couldn't. It's his. You keep it, sell it, you do whatever you want, that's fine, but it's still his." She stood up then, hesitated, almost sat down again, and then walked to the piano and sat down, resting her open hands on the keyboard. The music rest was covered with sheets of her own scrawled manuscripts, but she did not look at them.

For a long, terrible time nothing moved or sang in her.

It's gone. Gone with Shei'rah, the music, and Abuelita and everyone—just all gone. Never happened. None of it. Then, as though of its own accord, her right hand twitched in a sudden three-note flurry, and her left hand followed it with the long, slow-swelling glory of a moonrise in Shei'rah. Somewhere John Papas said, "*Hah!*" and said, "That!" and said something else in Greek. Joey pushed back the sleeves of Mr. Provotakis's bathrobe.

The music of Shei'rah came winging up under her hands,

welcoming her home. In the little shop the piano sounded like a full orchestra, exultantly embroidering strains born on the other side of the Border that cascaded through Joey, spilling through her so exultantly that she could not consider or contain them. She closed her eyes as she played, and not only saw Ko but smelled him, as she smelled the *javadur* fruit he brought her, and a forest floor soft with blue leaves. She walked with the Princess Lisha again, and clung to Touriq's back as he raced with the other young unicorns; she heard the brook-*jalla*'s laughter, like the sound of her stream, and the clicking of the *perytons*' teeth as they came slanting down on their prey. It was almost too much for her, and she almost made herself stop; but then her hands remembered the silence of the Lord Sinti, the stillness of a day spent in watching the little dragons, the raucous voices of a gang of *tirujai* singing something dirty, the dappled solitude of walking in Sundown Wood. If it was not quite the music of the Eldest, it brought them truly near to her, and when she did stop playing she covered her face, half-laughing in wonder. "Oh, I did get it, I *did*! Maybe not right, not really right, but even so. I *did* get Shei'rah!"

John Papas was nodding, grinning absurdly wider and wider. "Oh, yeah, you got something, all right, something like nothing else ever. Don't know what happens from here—we show it to a few people, maybe somebody plays it, records it, maybe yes, maybe not—but you got your Unicorn Sonata for keeps, kid. This doesn't leave you. This stays." After a moment, he added, "Thank you."

They sat smiling at each other in the dark music shop. John Papas finally turned and walked heavily to the front window. "I got to close up. You like to eat something disgusting at Provotakis's?"

Joey was putting her damp jeans back on. "No, thanks, I better go home." She picked up her battered backpack and joined him at the window. "It's getting dark way too early already. I hate this time of year." After a moment she added, "Especially when there's no other place I can be anymore."

John Papas put his arm on her shoulder. "Okay, Josephine Angelina Rivera. Okay now. That place, it's still there, right? Ain't like it stopped being—it's still *somewhere*, right? Okay, it moved, so what? So you move too. So you look around for that other place everywhere you go, starting now. There's unicorns all over everywhere, even Woodmont. You know that, I know that, maybe nobody else does. You look for them, you listen for the music, you listen for Shei'rah. It's somewhere, you'll find it, you want to find it enough. You got time."

Joey managed a smile. "I guess. Abuelita said I'd find it again. And I promised Touriq. See you Monday." She opened the shop door and started out.

John Papas called to her, pointing to her bare feet. "You gonna be all right like that? Here, I'll give you something, take a cab."

Joey laughed. "No, I feel like walking home. I just do."

"They'll notice," John Papas said. "Maybe not your folks, but your brother for sure. What you gonna say, how you lost your shoes?"

"I don't know," Joey said. "I'll worry about that later. Right now I'm sort of keeping an eye out for a skinny kid with really pretty eyes and an attitude. He's around here somewhere." She closed the door carefully behind her and started home.